The STEM Coaching

Learn how to promote STEM—science, technology, engineering, and mathematics—integration in your school district and increase student achievement. In this helpful, easy-to-read book, author Terry Talley sheds light on the key responsibilities and accountabilities of a successful STEM coach and offers a wealth of practical advice for those new to the position and for those who want to refine their skills.

You'll discover how to

◆ Build positive working relationships with teachers and faculty
◆ Organize professional development opportunities such as PLCs and book study groups
◆ Develop hands-on instructional strategies based on the needs of your students and the strengths of your staff
◆ Promote technological and scientific literacy to prepare students for success in the 21st Century
◆ Enhance student engagement using project-based learning and growth-based assessment models.

Designed to be read either as a step-by-step guide or as a reference, *The STEM Coaching Handbook* is loaded with insights and accounts from experienced STEM educators across the country. No matter your level of expertise, these tips will help you make your district's STEM program more effective for all students.

Terry Talley is Assistant Director for Professional Support at Accelerate Learning (created by Rice University), where she develops and provides science and STEM professional development for teachers and school districts.

Other Eye On Education Books Available from Routledge
(www.routledge.com/eyeoneducation)

The Mathematics Coaching Handbook:
Working with K-8 Teachers to Improve Instruction, 2nd Edition
Pia M. Hansen

The Literacy Coaching Handbook:
Working with Teachers to Increase Student Achievement
Diana Sisson and Betsy Sisson

Intentional Innovation:
How to Guide Risk-Taking, Build Creative Capacity, and Lead Change
A.J. Juliani

Hiring the Best Staff for Your School
How to Use Narrative to Improve Your Recruiting Process
Rick Jetter

An Educator's Guide to Dual Language Instruction
Increasing Achievement and Global Competence, K-12
Gayle Westerberg and Leslie Davison

Motivating Struggling Learners:
10 Ways to Build Student Success
Barbara R. Blackburn

Learning on Your Feet:
Incorporating Physical Activity into the K-8 Classroom
Brad Johnson and Melody Jones

Your First Year:
How to Survive and Thrive as a New Teacher
Todd Whitaker, Madeline Whitaker, and Katherine Whitaker

Crafting the Feedback Teachers Need and Deserve:
A Guide for Leaders
Thomas Van Soelen

Relationships That Work:
Four Ways to Connect (and Set Boundaries) with Colleagues, Students, and Parents
Adam Saenz and Jeremy Dew

Better Lesson Plans, Better Lessons:
Practical Strategies for Planning from Standards
Ben Curran

The STEM Coaching Handbook

Working with Teachers to Improve Instruction

Terry Talley

Routledge
Taylor & Francis Group

NEW YORK AND LONDON

First published 2017
by Routledge
711 Third Avenue, New York, NY 10017

and by Routledge
2 Park Square, Milton Park, Abingdon, Oxon, OX14 4RN

Routledge is an imprint of the Taylor & Francis Group, an informa business

Library of Congress Cataloging in Publication Data
Names: Talley, Terry, 1960-
Title: The STEM coaching handbook : working with teachers to improve instruction / by Terry Talley.
Description: New York : Routledge, 2017. | Includes bibliographical references.
Identifiers: LCCN 2016014474 | ISBN 9781138651029 (hardback) | ISBN 9781138651036 (pbk.)
Subjects: LCSH: Science--Study and teaching (Secondary) | Technology--Study and teaching (Secondary) | Engineering--Study and teaching (Secondary) | Mathematics--Study and teaching (Secondary)
Classification: LCC Q181 .T25 2017 | DDC 507.1/2--dc23
LC record available at https://lccn.loc.gov/2016014474

ISBN: 978–1–138–65102–9 (hbk)
ISBN: 978–1–138–65103–6 (pbk)
ISBN: 978–1–315–62500–3 (ebk)

Typeset in Palatino
by Saxon Graphics Ltd, Derby

Printed and bound in the United States of America by Publishers Graphics, LLC on sustainably sourced paper.

Contents

About the Author

Terry Talley holds undergraduate and graduate degrees in science and vocational education from the Mississippi University for Women and an EdD in Curriculum, Instruction, and Administration from the University of North Texas. She began her career as a secondary science teacher working with students in grades 6–9 for 14 years. Talley later served as a science teacher specialist, dean of instruction, UNT Professional Development School coordinator, pre-service teacher instructor and supervisor, and as science coordinator and supervisor for secondary science in two north Texas school districts. Talley served as an instructor in the College of Education at the University of North Texas, teaching online and on campus master's level education courses.

Dr. Talley joined Rice University to provide teacher outreach and professional development as the Program Manager for Professional Development with Accelerate Learning. With a focus on STEM—science, technology, engineering, and mathematics—education and an eye for current education research in STEM, Talley provides a perspective about STEM-based instructional practices for authentic STEM integration through a nationally recognized STEMposium. Prior to joining Rice, she was Program Manager and STEM Coach for the Southeast Regional Texas STEM Center at University of Texas Medical Branch (UTMB) and Beginning Teacher Induction and Mentoring (BTIM) Coach for the Texas Regional Collaboratives through the UTMB Office of Education Outreach.

Talley has received numerous awards for her work in science education, including Grapevine-Colleyville ISD Secondary Teacher of the Year, Texas Medical Association Teacher of the Year, Outstanding Texas Science Supervisor, and Cohort 5 member of the WestEd National Science Education Leadership Academy.

Foreword

Nothing is more joyful than to hear from a colleague you have known, admired, and respected for her contribution to our critical work in education and to learn that she, too, fell in love with the long studied, deeply researched and proven practice for achieving results—coaching. I have known Terry since she was a teacher and have had the privilege to watch her personally grow into an impactful leader and champion for all learning and particularly science. Terry has always been passionate about science, about high levels of learning for all kids, and doing whatever the job required with an exceptional level of excellence. It came as no surprise that she would be writing a book about STEM (science, technology, engineering, and mathematics)—to support the instructional coaches desiring to create deeper commitment, confidence, and passion for the impact that STEM work is having.

This handbook answers the "who," "what," "why," and whatever other question one may have about STEM. Regardless of the role one may play in the process this handbook offers a helpful and complete resource. As a professional executive coach and director of the Results Coaching Global coaching school, reading and learning from coaching books are right up at the top of my favorite things list with movies and popcorn.

The initial cheer in my reading came with the most critical standard and expectation as to what a STEM coach needs to be. This is the commitment to be what is needed, to do what is needed, and to become what is required—a consummate learner who lives for personal mastery. Allow me to lift high that standard.

A STEM coach also needs to:

◆ Be a campus thought leader and remain current in the research associated with instruction, assessment, and best practices in STEM education and trends.
◆ Be knowledgeable and skillful in the STEM-based practices of designing and implementing authentic problem-solving and design strategies.
◆ Be well versed in lesson design and use inquiry-based lesson planning as a means to shape the instructional focus to include a STEM-centered and student-centered focus.

◆ Be able to model instruction as a scaffold to build teacher confidence in a new instructional strategy.

◆ Provide formative feedback to teachers being mentored or coached.

◆ Avoid conducting or sharing teacher evaluations at all costs.

◆ Be an eager learner who is involved in a professional learning community of other STEM coaches.

◆ Conduct walk-through observations with administration and/or fellow coaches to observe for student engagement.

◆ Engage in professional dialogue with administration about STEM integration across all content areas.

◆ Be able to work with administration in developing a STEM mission and vision that reflects the views of stakeholders and community members.

◆ Plan and facilitate Professional Learning Communities (PLCs) that focus on reflection, student learning, and the instructional practices associated with STEM instruction.

◆ Plan, organize, and provide STEM professional development to teachers, campus leadership, and community members, including at conferences.

◆ Organize and facilitate campus STEM events that showcase STEM-based products and portfolios of student work.

◆ Act as a STEM ambassador to campus guests, parents, and community members who visit the campus.

This list begins the contract, along with the job responsibilities, for selecting and maintaining the best of the best in these critical roles. I can envision the conversation with each applicant and/or reviewing these with each returning STEM coach for the renewal and re-energizing of the work and role.

Being selected as a STEM coach has to be such an honor and it reflects the respect for one's knowledge and skills and passion towards STEM. The newest learning for any person in the position is that of being a coach. Coaching is a credentialed profession and carries with it competencies of practice, just as best practices in instruction. As one walks in this role, their commitment is also to growing in their role as "coach." The role itself requires something of us:

◆ The coach must believe in the ability and possibility within another. Just as teachers must believe in the students that are sent to their classes, the coach must believe in their teachers.

◆ The coach must know and continually articulate the standards and expectations of the STEM program and lift them up in each and every conversation. Not with obligation but with the belief that each teacher is on the journey to achieve each one.

◆ The coach must have highly effective communication skills that create a sense of safety and trust in each conversation and intentionally send the belief in the other person that they are working hard and continuously striving for the goals they have set.

◆ The coach must have confidence in their skills, feel the competence of their knowledge, and have the courage to "hold able" those they coach.

◆ The coach must engage in conversations that live the words of Susan Scott's Fierce Conversations: "Your central function is to engineer intelligent, spirited conversations that provide the basis for high levels of alignment, collaboration, and partnership at all levels throughout the organization and the healthier outcomes that go with them."

This handbook offers a complete tool for support and information that will serve the mission and magnify the vision of the STEM program. May this handbook and the work of coaches at all levels of the STEM program continually assess their progress on the magnificent journey to have high levels of math and science achievement of our students. And if the cornerstone of STEM learning is student engagement and exposure to innovation and design from instruction and learning that models real-world contexts, we will know it by our future. For we will surely measure our university graduates in science, technology, engineering, and mathematics and see it through their "dent in the universe." Each leader, each teacher, and each coach will make it happen by their passion, their commitment, and their belief in what is possible.

Kathryn Kee, M.ED, PCC
Owner/Partner Results Coaching Global
Author: *Results Coaching: The New Essential For School Leaders* ©2009
Author: *Results Coaching Next Steps: Leading for Growth and Change* ©2016
(in publication)

Acknowledgements

It is with gratitude to the teachers I have had the honor of mentoring and coaching over the years, and to those who mentored and coached me, that I write this book. I hope this handbook will serve as a challenge, that it will tempt you to reflect on your STEM instructional practices, encourage you to seek new ways to engage in professional learning, and to become a highly effective instructional coach for those you serve.

While writing this book I have called on the expertise and patience of many of my friends and colleagues. They shared their stories and insights about bringing STEM into the districts, campuses, and classrooms of the people they coached and mentored. My heartfelt gratitude is shared with Kathryn Kee, Dr. Jennifer Stotts, Dr. John Doughney, Dr. Joe Ferrara, Dr. Leslie Hancock, Dr. Marsha Ricks, Sharry Whitney, Denise Fisher, Joe Todd, Jodi Marchesso, Janelle McLaughlin, Debra Krikourian, Marisa Guzman, Kenya Wilson, Kyndra Johnson, Cindy Rubin, Sara Jones, Dillon Chevalier, Kristi Adams, Felecia Pittman, Kimberly Lane, and Tona Blizzard.

Thank you to my friend and proofreader, Sommer Fisher, who patiently worked with me through all the changes that occurred through the writing process of this book. Most importantly to my husband, Jerry Talley, thank you for being my most whole-hearted encourager and supporter as this project came into being.

Introduction

The decision to take the next step in your career and leave the classroom to become a STEM—science, technology, engineering, and mathematics—instructional coach is an emotional mix. Whenever you do make the decision, it will be for one of a variety of reasons: a personal challenge, the need for change, the desire to share what you know, or even for the stipend to offset your college loan debt. For whatever reason, you can look forward to a healthy dose of pride for being given elevated status among your peers, mixed with a sense of honor for recognition by the administration of your teaching practices and proven results with student achievement, softened by the sense of abandonment of your classroom, full of children, who brought you to education in the first place. But the hardest of all will be self-doubt and fear of not knowing how your peers will accept you in this new role, and if you will be able to be as successful with adults as you were with your students.

As an instructional coach, you may find that the role is loosely defined and it changes as quickly as the situations change on campus. You enjoy the freedom of not being tied to a bell schedule and each day is unique. But, because you are not assigned to a specific group of students, nor given a set schedule, you find you are often asked to step in when a substitute teacher doesn't show up or to tutor a group of students in preparation for a high-stakes test.

To have the most influence in your new role and the situation you have had the opportunity to fill, it is important to begin with a clear understanding of your role, your responsibilities, and the knowledge and skills required of a STEM instructional coach.

In this handbook we will identify the major tasks most STEM coaches have, the subsequent responsibilities for each task, the knowledge and skills you will need, and the coaching strategies that have been found to be effective in turning a traditional campus into a STEM-centered one. The important role of being a STEM instructional coach allows you to partner with your teachers, in challenging them to inspect their own practice, reflect on what is actually happening in their classrooms, and provide opportunities for them to sharpen their skills for the benefit of their students.

As a coach you will bump into some of the unwritten expectations, hidden challenges, and unfortunate consequences of being in the middle. That is the strange place where you are not an administrator with authority, but yet you are not a classroom teacher either. Although, at this time, a special degree or training is not required to be a STEM instructional coach, this handbook will share with you some resources and strategies found to be worthwhile in providing perspective and background about coaching. When you become more comfortable in your role and begin to adapt your coaching strategies for each teacher you serve, you will want join other STEM instructional coaches to share your insights and to learn from theirs. Just as each student is in need of a teacher who selects instructional strategies to meet their needs, so are the teachers you will mentor or coach.

How to Use This Book

The STEM Coaching Handbook is written for STEM coaches in all stages of their careers: from the classroom teacher who is considering the role and starting to look for STEM coaching jobs, to the experienced coach who is looking for ways to hone their craft or to move into another area of coaching.

If you are new to the idea of coaching STEM teachers, Part I will provide many ideas and insights into the experience and background knowledge you might consider. There is an ad for a STEM Coaching Position on page 63 that you might review before applying.

If you are a STEM coach with more experience it might suit you better to skim through Part I, meant for those newer to the role, and jump into Part II for some ideas and advice for working with administrators or in PLC groups.

If you are an administrator on a STEM campus, or considering providing a STEM program for your district, you may find Parts III and IV of this handbook useful when hiring STEM coaches, or for ideas to incorporate coaching into your STEM campus or program.

The book can be read straight through or read more like a reference where you flip to the sections you need.

Part I

STEM and the STEM Coach

Part I provides an overview of the phenomenon of STEM, the importance of having a clear vision when looking at instructional practices through the lens of STEM, as well as providing a perspective in the development of STEM as a force larger than just what is impacting our classrooms and school districts.

1

What Is STEM?
How Is It Different?

When you think of a campus where STEM—science, technology, engineering, and mathematics—is the focus, be it elementary or secondary, what are the things that come to mind? Does your vision include: labs with the newest state-of-the-art computers, with wall-mounted monitors and small groups of students working on their personal tablets or laptops collaborating in many locations around the campus; with a robotics team and science fair participants competing in state and national contests? Can you envision a STEM-focused campus where there is only one computer located on the teacher's desk connected to a projection system that is being used by a team of students sharing their findings and solution to a project-based learning challenge? Could your vision include a campus that within each core class teachers are focused on providing students with authentic yet age-appropriate problems to solve?

In my many conversations with district leadership, campus administrators, and teachers who want to become part of the STEM movement, their concerns are usually centered on the use of computers in each of the subject areas, with students having access to computers to continue their learning, and students using computers as the technology focus. It has occurred to me, through our discussions, that their concerns reveal misunderstanding about STEM. When asked, "What is STEM?" and "How does being a STEM campus make us different?" many were stumped by how to respond.

From the responses I have heard, there is never a clear description or understanding of the purpose of becoming a STEM-centered campus. Many teachers and campus leaders are lacking a clear understanding of how the four areas emphasized in STEM—science, technology, engineering, and mathematics—fit into a cohesive learning environment that makes a difference for students. Aside from providing greater computer access to students, how does adopting a STEM model make a difference to the traditional programs already in place and what would be the benefits to becoming STEM-centered?

As a STEM coach it was important for me to have a clear understanding of STEM to determine how to model and coach STEM-based teacher practices in order to impact teacher instruction and student achievement. How would this be different from what teachers and students were already doing? It is important to the classroom teacher to be able to plan lessons and implement STEM-centered learning opportunities for students' mastery of the content standards as well as the STEM-based skills. How does STEM influence student engagement and the work we ask them to complete? Will students be solving authentic problems and engineering practices in STEM activities to produce higher levels of mastery?

It is essential for the principal and campus leadership to understand STEM, so they are able to support it. What changes are needed for a STEM-based campus program to be effective and how do they encourage implementation of the instructional changes needed to become a STEM program? By having a clear understanding of STEM, campus leaders can become more focused when allocating the resources of time and funding, as well as planning for professional learning and instructional support. As the campus instructional leadership team, they need to become skillful in observing and assessing the quality of STEM instructional practices, for student engagement and for proficiency in STEM-based skills. They will need to be able to evaluate the students' depth of understanding and levels of achievement in mastery of content standards on assessments and how the STEM-based program impacted achievement scores.

Based on the National Science Foundation's report by the National Science Board called *Revisiting The STEM Workforce*, the focus is, "In particular, these insights reveal how STEM knowledge and skills enable both individual opportunity and national competitiveness, and how acquisition of STEM capabilities is increasingly vital to Americans' ability to participate fully in a 21st Century knowledge- and technology-intensive, global economy."

In the 1960s there was a crisis in science education. After the Russians launched Sputnik, a communication satellite, in 1957, many Americans felt current science instruction would not provide for the future engineers and scientists needed to compete in the space race. A focus on science instruction and science and math achievement gains provided an increase in the number of engineers and scientists in American universities. But, in recent generations, based on the comparative data from international assessments and the decreasing number of American engineering graduates, it has become apparent that we are again in a science education crisis. Recent discussions in social media and STEM studies report that China graduates more engineers than the United States. Although they have a larger population, the percentage of engineering graduates is higher than in the US. It is apparent, they state, that we need to grow our own capacity in STEM knowledge. Unless we do, our STEM-based economy will lag behind.

The current focus is about how we take STEM from the global market setting and incorporate that into our schools. How do we get more students excited about studying STEM fields, to go to college to major in STEM fields, and to persist to graduate with a STEM-based degree? We also need to figure out how to impact the groups in our population who are underrepresented in STEM fields. The ChangetheEquation.org website provides data and asks the question: If women make up 50% of the workforce, what factors are in play that bring only 25% into the STEM workforce? Enrollment data show that women do enroll in equal numbers in college STEM programs but they don't stay there. How do we change the dynamics? How do we become more open to women in STEM at the university level? Perhaps the solution is in empowering them at a younger age, engaging them in learning about the STEM fields, helping them to envision themselves as scientists and engineers, proving that they are capable, and supporting them so they can succeed.

According to Dr. Jennifer Stotts, a coach with Texas STEM, "STEM is not just about opportunities to move into engineering fields after college, but is about opening up learning opportunities and sophisticated problem-solving to all students. It is about inviting them to explore and engage in the interconnected real world in and out of the school, preparing them to be in the STEM pipeline, in line for STEM jobs. Right now there are not enough homegrown STEM scholars to fill the STEM jobs available and needed for our economy." To do this, Stotts states,

> We need to change how we teach. We have an entire populace engaged in the literacy of technology starting almost at birth. Right now there is more technology in our homes than ever before: smart home automation systems, self-vacuuming Roombas, programmable dishwashers and refrigerators, smart TVs, tablets, laptops, cell phones, etc. We already have a technology literate population when it comes to everyday devices. What we do not have is technology rich schools, instruction, and learning environments. In order to capture and engage students we need to grow

and expand this interdependent technological literacy into STEM literacy in schools; extend our reach to include mathematics, science, and innovation through engineering. Our goal is to learn how to naturally interface technology and innovation in schools as part of our non-negotiable preparation for STEM in their future.

In other words, according to the 2015 *Revisiting The STEM Workforce* report the students in our classrooms will eventually join the workforce. The STEM workforce is not made up of only scientists and engineers in Research and Development, or those who have received specific training to enter these fields, but includes those workers who use STEM knowledge and skills to "devise or adopt innovations or workers in technologically demanding jobs who need STEM capabilities." This report has hit the nail on the head when talking about STEM-focused programs. How well are we, as teachers and campus leaders, able to respond to these questions?

◆ Who are the STEM workers? Will our students be capable enough to be among them?
◆ What are the specific STEM knowledge and skills? Will our students be proficient in them before they graduate?
◆ Will our graduates be prepared to devise and adopt innovations and work with technology in ways that solve problems? Will they be STEM literate?

The director of STEM and Curriculum Innovation at the Lancaster Independent School District (ISD), Kyndra Johnson, shares with her team her views of STEM, which are holistic. She recognizes the importance of integrating STEM instruction across multiple disciplines. But, more importantly, she wants all instruction to be about choices, opportunities, and teaching through a STEM lens. STEM provides an academic foundation, which is flexible and adaptable. STEM is taught in a culture of engagement, authenticity, rigor, and content specificity. Yet, it is broad and it encompasses quite a few things that are not limited to science, math, engineering, and technology content. Johnson states,

My charge to the instructional team is to focus on STEM integration involving an awareness of careers and opportunities that students need to be exposed to before they leave as graduates; to provide a rich STEM background that allows graduates to leave with more than a diploma. That is our catalyst for change.

Johnson knows that not every student will be an engineer, a computer scientist, or a doctor; but all professions will require these skills and mindsets to be successful. It is important to understand that STEM is a culture of choice and partnership.

"We use STEM as filters and lenses. It is about the lenses we use in how we experience the world." According to Dr. John Doughney, the executive director of learning in the Grapevine-Colleyville Independent School District (GCISD) in the Dallas-Ft Worth Metroplex Area,

> STEM is one of the layers on top of all the content we want to have our students learn. I can be a better reader or writer through the lens of STEM. How do we think as designers and engineers in using the knowledge from the core content areas?

Doughney leads the cadre of learning liaisons and instructional coaches that are both district-deployed and campus-based for the successful implementation and integration of the district's targets and initiatives. Although not specifically directing the STEM initiative in GCISD, he supports the STEM coaches as they work with teachers and administrators in their roles on their two STEM campuses. According to Doughney:

> I am not an expert on STEM, but it is about mindset. How will I help kids to think certain ways to orient themselves towards innovation and discovery? STEM instruction is the perfect pathway to constructivism. They apply their knowledge with persistence, communication, and constructive feedback. These skills are not just STEM skills, all students benefit through their use.

As STEM coach and science curriculum coordinator in Lancaster ISD, Kenya Wilson, emphasizes, STEM is not just the components of the four core courses in STEM. The most important shift in STEM education requires that teachers guide students to analyze everything through the lens of STEM. Teachers need skills to integrate their content using the components of science, math, technology, and engineering. Eventually as they mature in STEM, teachers will automatically determine how STEM applies to all problem-solving or designing situations. They will include it in lessons for all contents such as: in dance class, planning an essay, or for debates in social studies. As a coach in this STEM-designated district in northeast Texas, Kyndra believes, "our whole district is learning how to make the shift." She supports all content area teachers so that as they teach their courses, they look for the ways to layer-in authentic, real-world problems that can be solved through the lens of STEM.

Joe Ferrara is the director at the University of Texas (UT), Dallas Institute for Instructional Excellence and at one time was a T-STEM coach at the UT Dallas Center for STEM Education and Research. Through his experiences working with middle and high schools, he developed a different way of looking at STEM implementation. "Many schools approach STEM by adding AP or dual credit classes to the math and science program or by starting a robotics program as afterschool enrichments." In his opinion, "Those approaches limit the number of students exposed to STEM and communicate a different message to teachers who do not teach traditional STEM subjects. In contrast, I have coached at new STEM academies, where the student body was selected through a lottery that opened the opportunity to learn in a STEM environment to all students and in all classes."

At the STEM academies, he worked with all teachers, not just those in math and science. "An ELA or social studies teacher should look different in a STEM Academy." According to Ferrara, "My thinking of STEM developed into a word, more like an adjective, and not an acronym. Not tearing it apart to add rigor, but looking for the common thread across all disciplines that ties them together." This allows teachers to implement the best instructional practices for their content areas with an authentic focus on STEM.

Denise Fisher is a learning liaison in Grapevine-Colleyville, a suburban school district in the Dallas-Ft Worth Metroplex area. She has also served as STEM coordinator and K-12 STEM coach in Texarkana ISD, TX and was an instructor in the STEM master's degree program at Texas A&M. As a colleague in STEM education, Fisher shared with me her insights into STEM at all four levels: as a classroom teacher who implemented engineering into her science classroom, as an MS campus STEM instructional specialist, as a district K-12 STEM coach, and as the district STEM coordinator. Fisher also served as a faculty member instructing in a STEM university program. Fisher strongly believes that:

> STEM is for students to become deeper thinkers and problem-solvers. We need to further prepare students for their futures and that means we need to build programs that are integrated, rigorous, yet relevant, and engaging. STEM career fields require this preparation prior to graduation for students to be college and career ready.

According to Fisher, STEM is an integrated approach to teaching and problem-solving. Students are learning by asking questions, seeking information, and engineering solutions. By using the Practices of Scientists and Engineers, as outlined in *A Framework For K-12 Science Education* (National Research Council, 2012), students and not just teachers are asking the intriguing questions and solving problems. Fisher thinks it is important for all students to have an inquiry-based mindset and to learn how to solve problems, by solving authentic, real-world problems. It is equally important for teachers who will facilitate this learning for students, to learn and teach this way. A teacher needs to be well versed in the engineering design process and all things STEM. Teachers need to be equally skilled in inquiry-based instruction. Fisher believes that "engineering can be the filter through which all content areas can be taught. Learning more about the new NGSS http:// www.nextgenscience.org/ and *A K-12 Science Framework* http://www. nextgenscience.org/framework-k%E2%80%9312-science-education helped to solidify this for me."

Pasadena Unified School District (USD) teacher on special assignment, Jodi Marchesso states, "For me, as a science major, STEM is important. I enjoy working with STEM programs because it is seeing the connection in everything." Her parents were open to encouraging her to pursue what she was interested in and so she chose to enroll in the arts in high school. Marchesso experienced a variety of skills through many perspectives. In turn she is able relate to a variety of teachers each with their own perspectives. Students need a chance to see how everything connects as well. In the research she has found about STEM education, it supports her view that STEM instructional practices help students to see the world as connected.

Jodi knows that STEM is also about problem-solving skills. It is her opinion that problem-solving is a soft skill that many students do not learn in school. Communication and collaboration should be taught in a school setting so when they are in the work setting they already have the skills mastered. Parents don't understand that mindset. They are concerned that their students are not being evaluated on their own efforts and content work. Within their STEM program teachers work to help parents understand the values of collaboration and other soft skills are just as important as their grades and transcripts.

According to Marisa Guzman, STEM coach in Katy ISD, STEM is more than just the standards-based content knowledge. It is learning to use critical-thinking skills. STEM adds value to a student's education because it improves their higher order thinking skills. Critical thinking and designing solutions are based in creativity and logic. These are higher cognitive level thinking abilities, which can be learned and practiced. STEM employers will be looking for employees who are critical thinkers. Coach Guzman states,

Because of recent articles that I have read and conferences that I have attended, my understanding of the workforce urgency for integrating science, technology, engineering, and math with current and future employers and employees has been clarified. A STEM focus now is the right thing for our students. I know teachers think this too, but the demands and routines of their classrooms stretch them very thin. It is my role as their instructional math and science coach to help them integrate these valuable STEM skills into their lessons. My teachers want support for mastering the instructional practices needed for their students to become critical thinkers and problem solvers.

Guzman's goal is for students to solve authentic problems like the ones they find every day, but not just using science or math, but finding a solution using the lens of engineering. The combined processes they use to solve these complex and sophisticated, yet age-appropriate problems will become the skills that they will be prepared to use in designing solutions and solving problems in their future lives and careers. That is STEM. STEM is about being prepared for a career and earning a living. That is economics.

Current and future jobs are being created in the areas of technology and engineering. In Marisa's opinion, these types of careers are project based and they will need to use their science and math content backgrounds in them. For students to learn the content in engaging and hands-on ways, she works with teachers to ensure their students are participating in well-designed work that is team-based and standards-based. They learn math and science while they are doing the projects. She states that it is also critical for students to learn to work together to complete their projects. Guzman feels it is important to learn these skills now for their future jobs, which will require collaboration with others to solve problems as a productive partner on a team.

Dr. Leslie Hancock is a high school instructional coach with GCISD. In her opinion, STEM is science, engineering, technology and math content. "But," she states, "it is a conglomeration of mathematics and science sub-disciplines, emphasizing skills students need to be successful in college majors and careers related to math and science. It pushes innovation to give opportunities to students that they would not have approached otherwise." She adds that there is an emphasis on literacy and vocabulary throughout math and science.

Being STEM-based goes well beyond meeting state curriculum standards and preparing for standards-based assessments. STEM is about being aligned to standards, but also authentic in the problems you ask your students to solve. It allows for autonomy in the student's voice and choice.

It is about solving problems. Students are better able to meet the College and Career Readiness Standards as addressed by *Common Core*, *ACT: Solutions for K-12 Education, College, and Career Readiness*, and *21st Century Skills* through STEM. Based on the 21st Century Skills described by the Partnership for 21st Century Skills (P21), STEM students are:

◆ Good communicators
◆ Good collaborators
◆ Information and technology literate
◆ Flexible and adaptable
◆ Innovative and creative
◆ Globally competent
◆ Financially literate.

Students in STEM-based programs not only gain the content requirements for mastery but they have gained the problem-solving and workforce skills that are essential for success after graduation. As they make decisions, in no matter what direction they choose, they will be literate scientifically, mathematically, and in solving problems.

When making the decision to become a STEM-based campus or district, having a complete understanding of STEM is important. But, more importantly, it is essential to understand the amount of change in the culture and instructional focus required to transform a traditional organization into one that is STEM-based. An honest evaluation of the district's or campus's desire to change and its capacity for change will be an indicator of how successful they will be as a STEM program.

The STEM coach's role becomes central in the implementation of a STEM-focus. In the next section we will look at several ways states, districts, and campuses have organized their instructional support systems to include STEM coaches. We will look at the strategies used for the successful transition to STEM instructional practices, higher levels of student engagement, and integration of problem-solving so that students gain STEM-based skills and higher levels of academic achievement.

2

The STEM Campus

Becoming a STEM campus is a transition that requires changes on many levels. It involves an understanding of what STEM is so that the transition creates a school that exemplifies the integration of all content areas and the skills and practices of a college- and career-ready student. It is also about changes in attitude that need to occur in those who are going to be involved in the transition.

The transition to a STEM instructional focus involves reaching and informing the many layers of the education community about the benefits of the transition as well as helping to address the mindsets of all who are involved—school board members, district administration, campus leadership, teachers, students, parents, community members, and business leaders—who will ultimately benefit from the shift. Teachers are the first string of implementers for STEM practices, and support is often required to help shift mindsets and instructional practices. To successfully transition into being an integrated STEM campus, the main focus should be on the teacher's mindset. District and campus leadership will need to work together to put together the strategic plan and support system to accomplish this large first step.

Because STEM has become the focus of many federal-level initiatives, funding from federal agencies has been made available through university and state education agency grants to increase the number of students in STEM programs. Districts and campuses applying for STEM grants have a myriad of stipulations and guidelines to follow in order to comply with grant directives. The rewards for being grant funded are the resources, training, and support that have been put in place through these agencies concerning STEM practices.

Districts and campuses that choose not to use federal or state grants can also develop extremely successful STEM programs, but additional funding may still be required. Often these funds are provided through sponsorship from industry stakeholders and other organizations that will benefit from STEM-educated graduates.

When considering the amount of funds provided to support teacher growth and development for the academic *achievement* of the students, it is important to take into consideration the quality of the outcomes for that level of spending. According to a 2015 study by The New Teacher Project (TNTP) called *The Mirage: Confronting The Hard Truth About Our Quest For Teacher Development*, the national average amount of funds in all budget items that are spent to impact teacher quality totaled over $18,000 per teacher. That takes into consideration things such as: principal and administrator time spent on teacher evaluations, walk-through observations, in-service days, district professional development (PD) days, the additional district staff hired to provide instructional support, substitute days so teachers can attend PD, the salaries of the district PD department, teacher and administrator conference registrations and travel, consultant fees, stipends paid to teachers to attend training, as well as the many other items that are intended to change teachers' instructional practice so that student achievement is impacted.

The decision to become a STEM district or campus is one not to be taken lightly based on the impact of the transition on the community and on the district's funds. But, once the decision has been made it is important to put the supports in place for its successful implementation.

3

The STEM Campus Instructional Leader

The principal, as the campus leader, has the responsibility of creating and maintaining the mission and vision of the STEM campus. By taking advantage of the many STEM-based leadership resources and networks available, the STEM leader on campus can set up and utilize a system of supports that move the campus's STEM initiative forward as well as successfully continuing progress on district initiatives. Through the careful and honest construction of the campus improvement plan (CIP), the principal and leadership team can put in place the checks and balances that provide for teacher learning as well as student growth in STEM content, skills, and academic achievement.

An Elementary Principal's Perspective on STEM and STEM Coaching

Cannon Elementary, a GCISD STEM school, is located in Grapevine, TX. Principal Tona Blizzard guided the STEM evolution of the campus four years ago. This is a campus in an amazing transition as a school-wide STEM-centered campus, as home to a dual-language program, and being Title I, based on the number of enrolled students who qualify for federal funded free or reduced-fee lunches.

Cannon received an accountability rating of Met Standard according to the School Report Card released by the Texas Education Agency (TEA) for the

2014–2015 school year. State accountability ratings were based on four performance indexes: Student Achievement, Student Progress, Closing Performance Gaps, and Postsecondary Readiness. According to Blizzard, they exceeded the target scores in all four categories, with a Student Achievement Index of 93! Becoming a STEM campus and focusing on quality instructional strategies are some of the factors Blizzard credits to the increasing scores on the School Report Card: "STEM at Cannon is a curricular program that integrates the concepts of STEM across the core content areas and electives as appropriate, with a strong emphasis on engineering and design thinking." It was important for their campus to clearly define STEM and their STEM focus because they wanted no misconceptions on the part of the community and parents about how their campus was implementing STEM.

The principal and staff at Cannon STEM want their students to be prepared for careers in the 21st Century, to be critical thinkers, problem solvers, and solution finders of authentic problems. It is an economic imperative that puts the onus on her staff to prepare their students for careers that require STEM skills. Blizzard states that their approach was not: We are going to teach and then do STEM. It was also not about just teaching an engineering design process and building prototypes. Accordingly, she states:

> STEM-based learning does not happen that way. It needed to be integrated. STEM at Cannon is teaching kids how to think and think through a problem. It is thinking about everything through a STEM lens and using it to learn across all content areas. STEM skills cannot be taught in isolation and be effective.

Cannon's STEM-based initiatives align perfectly with the district's initiatives, according to Blizzard. The district clearly outlined its strategic plan in a document entitled LEAD 2021. The district's strategic plan name is an acronym for Leading Excellence –Action Driven. It was initiated in 2011 as the product of the collaborative efforts between the district and the community. It was established to guide the progress of the district objectives and strategies on which the district leadership would focus for the next ten years.

Each campus leader works on implementation of LEAD 2021 through the development of the campus improvement plan (CIP). The Cannon CIP and the STEM program support the development of students in each of these outcomes:

◆ Problem solvers
◆ Effective communicators
◆ Collaborative learners

◆ Global citizens
◆ Self-regulated learners.

The focus on learning strategies was in perfect alignment with LEAD 2021. For example, in Cannon's CIP, www.gcisd-k12.org/Domain/1428, for District Goal 6: Strategy #3, CIP Objective #2 there are three strategies associated with STEM-based learning:

Goal 6: STRATEGY #3—We will transform from a teaching platform to a learning platform by designing engaging, differentiated work for students towards the accomplishment of the GCISD mission and strategic objectives.

Performance Objective 2: 100% of Cannon students, in all student populations, will be students who think critically, innovate, and invent to solve real-world problems.

Strategy Description 1) Teachers will design STEM-based instruction focused on essential content and skills.

Strategy Description 2) Teachers will integrate STEM content areas by utilizing a Project-Based Learning instructional model, and teaching the design process utilized in elementary engineering curriculum.

Strategy Description 3) The GCISD Framework for Learning—Guiding Principle III will be utilized in PLCs to ensure that instructional design supports TEKS [standards] and all aspects of Cannon's STEM program.

To help each campus meet its objectives and goals the district's Curriculum and Instruction Division trains and deploys campus-learning liaisons. Liaisons are instructional coaches assigned to each campus who do most of their work through coaching and facilitating PLCs. Although not a STEM-based person, the campus liaison at Cannon has a deep background in the humanities and English Language Arts (ELA). According to Blizzard, she is also a tremendous learner and fully understands Cannon's STEM focus and STEM integration design. She operates through the lens of ELA. Blizzard is impressed with her skills and perception for thinking like this. "If I had a coach like her when I was in the classroom, it would have changed the way I thought." All the humanities courses are now impacted for the better. It is her strengths as an instructional specialist, focusing on best practices, that allow her to get through to teachers.

The district's STEM coach is their go-to person for science content knowledge and STEM-strategies. According to Blizzard, the instructional coach and the STEM coach are the perfect bookends for STEM and literacy. It is their mindsets, thinking as learners, and being passionate about student success that make for a perfect fit for the campus.

Cannon used the *T-STEM Design Blueprint*, http://www.tstemblueprint. org/, that was adapted for its elementary campus as the guiding document for the development and organization of the campus. It is organized into benchmarks to guide Cannon's growth. The staff developed a profile of a role-model STEM teacher to help provide a lens for the hiring process, but they found it also helped to frame their expectations for their faculty. It is used to define what PD they need and to help them get the supports they need to continue to improve their practice.

STEM teachers at Cannon have been trained in the inquiry model, based on the model used by the Exploratorium—the Museum of Science, Art and Human Perception, located in San Francisco, CA (a leader in inquiry education). Teachers understand it conceptually and utilize it in their classrooms so students can experience inquiry through project-based learning (PBL). Additionally, Blizzard schedules several inquiry PD days with new staff and as a refresher for veteran teachers. Teachers also annually receive training in PBL, engineering, uncovering student misconceptions, and technology.

In addition to the instructional coach, technology support is provided by the district-deployed technology coaches who co-teach with teachers. The majority of Cannon teachers have gone through the Code.org training program to get a background for the "why" that coding is important for kids.

Engineering was the next biggest thing. The Cannon STEM teachers began using *Engineering Is Elementary (EIE)* from the Science Museum of Boston. In Blizzard's opinion, "*EIE* did a nice job of helping us learn how to teach engineering at the elementary level and we used this resource heavily at the beginning of our program." As the STEM program evolved, the teachers wanted deeper and more integrated content, with more authentic literature connections.

As a certified *EIE* trainer and STEM consultant, Liz Parry has proven to be a valuable resource for Cannon teachers as they implement engineering. She is a former mechanical engineer, and has translated a real-world perspective of engineering into a classroom experience that models not only how to integrate the 21st Century Skills needed by the workforce, but also use of the practical skills of problem solving. She is skillful in engaging the interests of a diverse group of learners.

A Secondary Principal's Perspective on STEM and STEM Coaches

Dr. Marsha Ricks is the principal of the Ball High STEM Preparatory Academy, a school-within-a-school program in Ball High School on Galveston Island. As the founding principal, she established the culture for STEM learning and student achievement. The creation of the Ball STEM Academy was part of a national initiative to promote STEM with K-12 students and a culture of scientific thinking. It entailed raising the rigor in math, science, and technology for teachers and students and promoting a specific way of thinking about science and math for all teachers and educators.

Ricks believes it was her role to help the community and parents understand the need for growth in STEM careers. Global trends show lost ground in science since the time after Sputnik. US students have not kept up with other countries in science and math. Globally we are behind in other areas and skills. According to Ricks, the purpose of STEM is to rethink how we engage students and education systems in those areas that have a global impact. The world is moving forward and the US needs to focus on how it re-engages its students in STEM fields in order to keep up.

According to Ricks, STEM is reaching beyond the four content areas; it encompasses all fields and in all occupations. When looking at the local community and the stakeholders the school serves, she states, "I think STEM is found in many areas; not just in those narrowly identified because they are directly related to the S, T, E, M in the name." When she first started formally planning to establish the STEM academy at Ball High, she referred to the *T-STEM Design Blueprint* as her guide. It stated that her academy needed to offer internships to students as part of the STEM capstone requirements. The underlying premise for the internship was that it needed to be in a STEM profession:

> This is my own twist on it. I know Galveston has the University of Texas Medical Branch (UTMB) as a resource to reach out to for biomedical-based professional internships. But, we also have Texas A&M University Galveston (TAMUG) for marine and environmental issues and Corps of Engineers for engineering. I have a population of students that cannot be forced into a profile or pipeline. They want choice; we need to provide internships in fields that interest them. Internships in science research, math or other STEM areas do not suit them. We accomplish this with our internship program by allowing them to intern in any field: lawyers, teachers, etc. As long as they find the STEM in it and determine the link where STEM is promoted they receive the OK to proceed.

So she was able to reinforce within her STEM program that STEM is everywhere and not just in the fields of science, engineering, technology, or math. Science and math are in STEM-based fields and also found in every profession. STEM makes students more knowledgeable and learning more authentic. When looking for STEM literacy, it is found in architecture, medicine, and beyond. If teachers and students have a STEM mindset, it is not hard to find the STEM connection.

Ricks' responsibilities for the district's initiative for student achievement gains were challenged by the fact that her T-STEM academy was not a magnet school, but one that chose its student population through a lottery for 100 students each year. Almost 50% of her students were considered at risk of failing academically or dropping out of school, and many had not taken any advanced programs prior to enrolling in this rigorous program. Through careful selection of her staff in the hiring process, professional development, and an embedded philosophy of STEM, she was able to establish a safety net for the STEM academy students.

To help her meet this challenge, the school district employed instructional specialists to provide support for her STEM teachers in instructional strategies and mentors for her new staff. But the support staff provided by the district were limited in their abilities to assist in coaching for STEM-based practices. The T-STEM organization provided a STEM coach, Dr. Jennifer Stotts, to help her in organizing and guiding the campus operations in meeting the criteria of the *T-STEM Design Blueprint*. Stotts provided PD in STEM practices and consistently talked about the overarching STEM focus of their instruction. She helped Ricks to gain expertise in observing and coaching for implementation. As a result, Ricks saw more of the STEM philosophy and practices being infused into her teachers' lessons. The annual state assessment scores for Ball High STEM Academy were well above the district in all content areas.

Stotts was able to provide several different levels of support to Ricks: to establish the academy, to maintain it, and to keep it growing with sustainability. She met with Ricks monthly and also met with teachers. Substitute teachers would take the STEM teachers classes for half days in the mornings or afternoons so they could meet with Stotts to learn how to build a STEM-based learning culture and how to embrace a mindset for working with students who would need many specific supports in order to succeed and excel. Stotts worked through roadblocks and helped teachers to see the value of overcoming them. It was almost into their second year until it became "the normal" and the campus embraced it. Teachers maintain the culture and share the culture with new members of their faculty as the campus grows.

As the academy became larger and more grade levels were added, the STEM teachers and academy students anticipated sharing the culture, traditions, and routines associated with the STEM format. But with growth, STEM coaching was needed for different reasons such as a source for new ideas and for continued growth. Stotts did not visit as frequently and much of the time spent during her visits was about accountability and brainstorming for new ways to become more effective and efficient.

The role of coaching teachers fell to Ricks as an administrator and learning leader who was able to provide curricular resources, to send teachers to STEM professional learning, and to help them grow through self-directed learning. Occasionally she was able to bring in consultants from national STEM organizations. The STEM academy faculty met regularly for PLCs in grade level teams to build and grow their skills. They also grew in expertise in looking for facets of their content areas that blend in studies for STEM integration. As a group they could support the students they had in common to be successful while looking at the whole child from each of their content perspectives.

The nearby T-STEM Center at UTMB also provided a STEM coach to work with new teachers using a Beginning Teacher Induction and Mentoring Grant (BTIM). Through observations, frequent coaching, and participating in the BTIM PLCs, Ball Prep STEM Academy welcomed its new faculty members while maintaining its role-model status for implementation of STEM practices within the T-STEM organization.

When Ricks was asked what areas of support a campus-based STEM coach could provide for her campus, she articulated the following list:

1. Acclimating new teachers to a STEM culture
2. Instructional strategies to differentiate for struggling learners
3. Technology integration into classroom routines and instructional practice
4. Encouraging a growth mindset in faculty and staff to deal with the challenges of working with a very diverse student population
5. Instilling advanced academic strategies for the increased rigor required for college and career readiness
6. Motivating reluctant learners to strive through a growth mindset
7. Integrating PBLs as a method to deliver curriculum rather than as added programs twice per year.

4

Who Needs a Coach?

When I think about coaching and where it occurs most often, I think about sports. If someone were asked to make a list of star basketball players, I would guess that Michael Jordan would be on it. In my mind, he is the epitome of a star athlete. Did you know that up until his retirement he had a personal coach that worked with him to keep his skill set fine-tuned? Hard to imagine isn't it? He has played the sport for over 30 years. But, when you consider he was in the NBA from 1984 until his last retirement in 2003 as a player, he had to stay on top of his game. He knew he needed someone to watch his moves, strategies, and actions, and to provide feedback to keep him fine-tuned. Considering that the younger and quicker players, who studied his every move, would have moved well past him, he chose to use his coach to stay ahead of them. Jordan would not have stayed the best in the league for so long without his tremendous work ethic, competitiveness, and willingness to work on his game to continually improve. So why wouldn't a teacher want or appreciate a coach?

In my own personal experience, as a science teacher and Teacher on Special Assignment with my school district, I had the opportunity to work with Kathy Kee when she was Assistant Superintendent for Curriculum and Instruction in Grapevine-Colleyville ISD. She provided professional development to district teachers and leaders who were considering using cognitive coaching (CC), developed by Arthur L. Costa and Robert J. Garmstron , as their alternative evaluation process. I attended the sessions, was impressed, and energized. I reread all our training materials, practiced positive presuppositions on colleagues and my husband, worked on framing questions so that responses could be more thoughtful, and I practiced listening with friends without it becoming autobiographical. But, it wasn't until my colleague Mary Arthur, the campus ELA interventionist, and I actually put CC into practice that I saw the real power of it.

Mary and I coached each other's plans for the lessons each of us would teach while the other observed. It was a bit awkward, almost mechanical at first, but we soon fell into a rhythm. We used coaching to help each other decide what we wanted our lesson to accomplish, what to observe, and what data to collect; we then observed each other's classes. For our final session we went together to share our portfolios and debrief our observation data with our campus principal. We shared with him a few questions he might want to use in our coaching session because he was not fully trained in CC as yet; but he caught on quickly.

Not only were Mary and I thoughtful in our responses, we recognized how much we grew in our thinking. We realized how differently we planned for teaching and learning, and towards impact on student learning. As campus and district leaders, our roles are to help teachers to consider more thoughtfully their instructional decisions. We began to anticipate the impact CC could have on the ways others added depth to their own thinking about teaching and learning.

Consider the TNPN research and findings in the 2015 report *The Mirage: Confronting the Hard Truth About Our Quest for Professional Development*. Among the group of teachers studied, 83% rated themselves as proficient or role model. When compared to the actual ratings given to them on their last evaluation, 65% were rated at the novice or gaining skills level. The article went on to state that many in the sample were teachers who had been in the classroom five years or longer and had reached a plateau in their instructional effectiveness. It made me think about the teacher evaluation systems that were used when I was teaching. None were written to challenge me to improve my practice or to want to grow professionally; I just needed to be proficient. But, it was not until my tenth year of teaching, when I was introduced to Cognitive Coaching, that I realized I needed to work on my instructional practices if I was going to continue to grow professionally for the benefit of my students' learning.

In their 2014 book, *Five Levers To Improve Learning: How To Prioritize For Powerful School Results*, Tony Frontier and James Rickabaugh point out that, "A classroom with an effective teacher is associated with growth in student learning at a rate that is three times greater than that in a classroom with a low-performing teacher." It is imperative to establish a culture of learning and growth on the campus for everyone who is impacting student achievement. Coaching has great potential in this area.

For a variety of reasons the commitment and motivation of some teachers and campus leaders to continue to learn and adapt instruction to the needs of the learners in their room is no longer there. Sometimes for stressed teachers the need to differentiate becomes a burden rather than a challenge. For others perhaps, they just don't know what they don't know because they never faced that challenge before and now in a new situation they have no idea what to do. Sometimes teachers feel overwhelmed. Using instructional strategies that were successful with former students, but are not successful in meeting the needs of their current students, may cause this. They don't have the time or an understanding of how to adapt or adjust for their students' various instructional needs. Finally, perhaps they have been told they are "good enough" for so long that they begin to believe they no longer need to work at improving their practice.

Without a professional development strategy in place that can differentiate for the individual needs of each teacher, the predictions of *The Mirage* TNPN publication will remain true and unchanged. In the journal *Education Week*, Mike Schmoker comments "to achieve a transformation reformers will need to review the full scope of professional development, including training, workshops, teacher collaboration and instructional coaching with two vital questions in mind":

1. Are we training teachers in methods that are among the very best practices that exist today—those with the strongest, most enduring evidence base and pedigree?
2. Are we observing those principles most essential to effective training—in particular, for example, that even rough mastery requires a sustained focus on a severely limited list of practices, with multiple opportunities for frequent monitoring, feedback, and follow-up training?

Coaches are already part of the support system provided by district and campus leadership. As Chip and Dan Heath state in *Switch: How To Change Things When Change Is Hard* (2010), a coach as a leader "points to the destination and clears the path" so that teachers can focus on the changes that are necessary.

If the current level of PD and instructional specialist assistance is not creating the changes that are needed, perhaps a new model is what is needed. When districts and teachers are challenged to change their choice of actions to positively impact student learning and achievement, implementing a coaching system to provide the support and structures for deeper thinking and implementation success needs to become the norm. STEM coaches who have an interdisciplinary view through a STEM lens for content integration and a mastery of highly effective instructional strategies are needed. There is a need for STEM coaches who can create a safe and who has risk-free space for thinking, learning, practicing, and fine-tuning the content and STEM skills and instructional strategies that will turn every teacher into the role-model teachers they perceive themselves to be.

A Portrait of a STEM Coach

Can you remember the person who had the greatest impact on you when you were a new teacher? Did they make you feel competent and capable? Were they kind enough to tell you when you didn't quite hit the mark? What were their traits and skills? Did they make a difference in your choice to stay in teaching? Do you feel you had a good or bad relationship with them?

I recall my first year teaching in a public school in San Antonio, TX and my department chair took me under her wing and became such a valuable person in my professional life. She shared her lesson resources, talked me through my lesson planning, showed me how to organize a lab, and even sat in with me during my first parent–teacher conference. She was a really busy person as department chair, and didn't have a lot of time to give me, but gave me what she could. To this day, I am still appreciative of the support Jean Hopkins provided and want to share it forward.

While attending Beginning Teacher Induction and Mentoring (BTIM) training several years ago, the trainer asked us what we thought were the most important traits for a coach and mentor. We compiled the list below. I wrote them down in the front of my personal planner so I wouldn't forget. Although not an official survey, our list was not too different from the traits I found listed in the many books I have read while doing research for this book. Coaches and mentors are:

◆ Trustworthy
◆ Good listeners
◆ Caring
◆ Available
◆ Knowledgeable
◆ Non-judgmental
◆ Observant
◆ Good communicators
◆ Confidantes
◆ Honest
◆ Reliable.

With each one of these coaching traits we generated, there was a story or a comment about coaches and mentors who were the opposite of what we stated. I heard one story of a coach who challenged a brand-new teacher to try a new strategy. As a novice the teacher wasn't comfortable doing it. But, she finally agreed that she would try it. She practiced a little and prepared a lot. Unfortunately, she was failing miserably when the principal walked in. She later found out he had been invited by her coach to watch as she used it with her students. What he saw was not what she wanted him to see and it later appeared on her evaluation. She said she didn't even want to meet with her coach again after that. According to Dr. Hancock, an instructional coach at Grapevine High School in the Grapevine-Colleyville School District, Grapevine, TX,

> When you evaluate—the relationship is impacted. We are thinking partners with them. We can be reflective, but we are not going to put them at risk if they try something and it doesn't work. There is no punishment for not being successful the first time, only growth. Even when you're wrong, you're right. You've learned something.

Have you considered the impact you could have as a coach or mentor? Do you have the skills to maintain a trusting relationship with the person you want to help? What traits and skills do you have that qualify you to be a coach? In this next section the qualifications, experience, and training of highly effective coaches will be discussed.

Dr. Leslie Hancock shared with me her philosophy of coaching, which struck a chord with my own:

> Our teaching philosophy is based on past experiences. We may encounter success and deem change unnecessary. But, if we aren't growing we are dying. Good is the enemy of great. Educators can never rest on our laurels and state that we are doing "good enough." The best teachers are those that constantly work to refine their craft. This is a challenging endeavor because teaching is a personal thing. When you ask teachers to be reflective and enter into a critical conversation with you about their teaching practice, it is an extremely delicate undertaking. Teaching is an act of caring. When you suggest a way to enhance their practices, they may interpret you are saying they are not caring enough.

An effective teacher has a well-developed portfolio of additional professional learning in instructional strategies well past their bachelor's degree. These trainings and professional development are essential for the teacher to learn differentiated strategies so all students receiving their instruction can be successful.

An effective coach must also have a well-developed portfolio of coaching strategies. In order to be appropriate for the developmental level and learning needs of each teacher, the coaching sessions and professional development could require a range of strategies. A coach understands the needs of the campus for a variety of professional learning opportunities at many levels: from the novice teacher, to the highly experienced, effective teacher. If PD and coaching are expected to meet the STEM teachers' needs then the coach needs to ensure the structures used cause each teacher to reflect and think more deeply about their effectiveness as a teacher and their use of highly effective instructional strategies.

These opportunities may include: mentoring induction-year and first-year teachers, coaching experienced teachers who are new to a grade level or content area, setting up PD sessions, and facilitating PLC groups to investigate STEM best practices.

A STEM coach also needs to:

◆ Be a campus thought leader and remain current in the research associated with instruction, assessment, and best practices in STEM education and trends

◆ Be knowledgeable and skillful in the STEM-based practices of designing and implementing authentic problem-solving and design strategies

◆ Be well versed in lesson design and use inquiry-based lesson planning as a means to shape the instructional focus to include a STEM-centered and student-centered focus

◆ Be able to model instruction as a scaffold to build teacher confidence in a new instructional strategy

◆ Provide formative feedback to teachers being mentored or coached

◆ Avoid conducting or sharing teacher evaluations at all costs

◆ Be an eager learner who is involved in a PLC of other STEM coaches

◆ Conduct walk-through observations with administration and/or fellow coaches to observe for student engagement

◆ Engage in professional dialogue with administration about STEM integration across all content areas

◆ Be able to work with administration in developing a STEM mission and vision that reflects the views of stakeholders and community members

◆ Plan and facilitate PLCs that focus on reflection, student learning, and the instructional practices associated with STEM instruction

◆ Plan, organize, and provide STEM professional development to teachers, campus leadership, community members, and at conferences

◆ Organize and facilitate campus STEM events that showcase STEM-based products and portfolios of student work

◆ Act as a STEM ambassador to campus guests, parents, and community members who visit the campus.

Where Do STEM Coaches Come from?

There are many pathways to becoming a STEM coach. Jodi Marchesso, a teacher on special assignment in Pasadena USD, shared her interesting journey. "It was all by accident that I got into education," she said. Originally, she went to college to be an exotic cat veterinarian and did graduate with a degree in biology. She got a job working at a wildlife park in South Dakota that raised North American animals like bears, wolves, cats, etc. After being there for a while she realized her career in wildlife care was a dead end. There was no career growth and as a tourist business it only provided income for 10 months a year. She would need a second job! So, she went back to college and earned a degree in education.

Marchesso was an emergency certified teacher with no experience, who had the opportunity to teach in many interesting settings. Each experience added to her wealth of knowledge and preparation for coaching teachers who are now in similar situations. Jodi first taught in small rural schools with low-income families that lacked diversity and then on a reservation in South Dakota, with five daily secondary science preps, with high-need students, while coaching volleyball. When she moved to Pasadena there were many transitions for her such as going from a grades 7–12 teaching assignment to teaching only seventh graders. Her class size went from 24 students to 38–46 students. The biggest change was in the needs of her students.

Marchesso moved from a teaching assignment with little diversity and an average socio-economic status (SES) to high diversity with the majority being low SES with 90% minority. She had a humbling experience as she kept trying to do what she did in the past with little success. The principal told her, "What you were doing is not best for students." She was warned that if she did not change her instructional practices he would have to let her go. "I knew I needed to change—so I tried everything I knew, but it didn't work."

As a final resort, Marchesso enrolled in an online master's degree in education while she was still teaching.

> The class that changed me the most was Educational Psychology. In the master's level course we discussed learning theories and I tried them out on my students to see what worked. Constructivism worked the best

and I started shifting. I implemented *Layered Curriculum* by Kathy Nunley and it changed my classroom environment immediately with differentiating learning for diverse learners.

Marchesso used this additional knowledge and gained enough experience to become a PLC leader for the National Education Association (NEA) Literacy Across America grant. She prepared and provided professional development sessions. She learned how to observe classroom instruction and watch for strategies that were working for teachers as they implemented changes in their instructional practices. As a result, her decision to become an instructional coach was made.

The district offered Marchesso a position and provided the opportunity for her to attend West Ed leadership training. While still improving as a Teacher on Special Assignment, she grew in her leadership role and is now instrumental in district-level science curricular changes. One change included her choice to implement STEM instructional strategies and to provide coaching for teachers to help them in their transition. Her role is to work with teachers as they are adjusting to the many demands that are placed on them for innovative teaching in initiatives, STEM-based learning, and increasing student achievement.

Dr. Leslie Hancock, who began as an English teacher wearing two hats at the same time, being both teacher and instructional coach, shared another interesting pathway. The 2015–2016 school year was her first full year as liaison between the district and the campus, with high school teachers:

> I chose to be a coach because I had a humbling experience in my career. Up until that point I felt I didn't need a coach, but when I joined the district, one was assigned to me. I thought I knew it all. I didn't see a value in coaching. I thought, "Who are you to tell me how to improve my practice? I'm not broken." Then, after having a baby, I had a sense of renewal. I decided to go all in before I wrote off the coaching model. I worked with a coach and I began to believe in the process. Now I say, "Don't knock it until you try it." Having those conversations with a coach was important to me. That epiphany helped me to know where the teachers I work with are coming from. Some of the best coaching conferences I have had are centered on that same idea.

Janelle McLaughlin, a STEM consultant, was an elementary teacher, mostly in second grade, for 14 years. When asked what kept her in the classroom all that time, she admits it was her students. She tracks her former students through their schooling and the last group she taught is now in seventh grade. She loves the learning process, watching the light bulbs of thoughts and ideas come on and the joys of discovery. She saw that in her students and now sees it in adults.

McLaughlin left the classroom to become the district curriculum director over all content areas and was responsible for leading and coordinating the district instructional professional development: "I enjoyed researching the various professional development opportunities available and digging into the research of those who offer advice and consulting."

Now as a professional coach and consultant McLaughlin works with school districts all over the US. In this role she creates partnerships with schools through a professional learning plan. McLaughlin works with cohorts within each organization to integrate best instructional practices into their operations. A typical cohort has around 20 teachers. The first step is about setting up the infrastructure for success and working with teachers through whole-group workshops to create an awareness of what they can accomplish. Then she begins meeting one-to-one with teachers, within each cohort, to coach and model the use of the strategies:

> I did not receive any specific training to be a coach. I learned as I went along, drawing on past experiences as a teacher and administrator. I learned from my mistakes and successes. I attended many professional development trainings as a teacher and as a curriculum director, so I am able to draw from all of those.

In McLaughlin's endeavors as a consultant and coach, she finds that she needs to stay sharp in her knowledge and skills, constantly reading, researching, and applying what she knows about building positive relationships. She has partnered with highly effective coaches who mentor, share resources, and allow her to ask many questions.

Sharry Whitney, a STEM professional development manager with Accelerate Learning, has held many roles in STEM education—seventh grade science teacher, campus instructional coach, district science specialist, and science curriculum supervisor—and has been in education for over 28 years. Her last teaching assignment was in seventh grade science in Lewisville ISD, a large school district in the Dallas-Ft Worth Metroplex. She was department chair and was part of the campus leadership team that provided the teacher perspective to decisions made by leadership.

Whitney chose to move out of the classroom because of an opportunity to become a campus instructional coach:

To me it was a way to impact the instructional practices of teachers as a larger way to impact student learning. As a teacher I had limited influence over student learning. I was influencing the thinking and learning of my 150 students every day. But as a coach, I would have an opportunity to multiply that through the best practices used by teachers by reaching X number of teachers times X number of students daily. My goal was to spread the word about the increased opportunities for student success through their teachers using best instructional practices.

With no regrets, she left the classroom, but does admit to missing the direct interactions with students. "I miss the relationships that were built through learning and actually watching them change and grow intellectually."

While in her role as campus instruction coach, Whitney was offered an opportunity to move into administration and become a curriculum specialist at the district level. At the time she had begun working on a master's degree in education administration and curriculum. After three years at the district level, her supervisor retired and she was offered the position of Secondary Science Supervisor. With her degree in hand, she knew the next step she wanted to take was not to become a principal but to become a curriculum supervisor. Her goals were to remain in the science curriculum and to work towards improving science instruction.

Whitney realized she had a depth of understanding in science content. She also had developed the skill set needed to be an effective supervisor through her degree and because she was mentored and coached by the current supervisor. According to Whitney, her supervisor shared all that she had developed and her insights into their development. By her observing the processes she used for the operation of the secondary science department and the coaching she provided, the transition was seamless. Whitney also found that the coaching skills she developed and used as a campus instructional coach were called up regularly as she worked with teachers on all the middle and high school campuses she served and with administrators on their campuses.

Math–science coach and instructional specialist Marisa Guzman's teaching career began as a bilingual pre-K through first grade teacher. She moved to the Houston area and began to teach fourth grade. Guzman found she liked teaching older students and became versed in combining science and math. The Rice University Elementary Model Science Lab (REMSL) program invited her to participate in its inquiry-based PD program. It was in this program that Guzman began to develop her skills in the 5E constructivist model for teaching science and math to students in kindergarten through fifth grade.

Guzman learned that the 5E instructional model provided an opportunity to bring inquiry learning into her classroom. The 5E model follows a pathway to initially engage students in the concepts to be studied through a short simple event that hooks students into wanting to learn more. They explore the concept through hands-on experiences before formal instruction. Students explain to their peers and teacher what they learned through their explorations and then through an elaboration to apply their learning to real-world scenarios or situations. By using the 5E model to learn science concepts, students are engaged in Constructivism, which is an educational philosophy of allowing students to build their conceptual understanding of a phenomenon as they are engaged in it. By exploring with their peers during hands-on learning experiences, and explaining to their teacher what they observe and learn about the phenomenon, students are able to construct a deeper understanding about science concepts.

Guzman's involvement in the REMSL program opened her eyes to the curiosity and excitement that science generates in students. When she used the instructional strategies she learned with her own students, she saw them become willing to dig deeper, wanting to learn more, asking important questions, and searching for answers. Working with such high-quality instructors at Rice opened her eyes to the value of professional learning and she wanted to learn more. Guzman says:

> The stronger I became in science the stronger my students became in science and math. Because we were building those higher-order thinking skills, the data, charts, and graphs led more to math. My students were thinking outside the box. Instead of trying to solve it just one way the students were not giving up. They searched other ways to make it work! The students began to feel comfortable with using more than one way to solve and verify problems.

As a result of her professional learning experience and the instructors in her program, Guzman enrolled in a master's degree program and earned a degree in Curriculum and Instruction with an emphasis in science: "I wanted to become an instructional coach after the REMSL program." Guzman stated that she was on fire and wanted to share all her learning with her grade level co-workers.

The instructors expanded and stretched her knowledge of science to other grade levels and she became eager to share with other grades on her campus as well. When the principal learned of her excitement, he encouraged her to apply for the instructional coach's position on her campus. Although she didn't get that position, she was hired for another campus as a coach. She has seen the results of her coaching begin to grow. As she coaches through the STEM lens she has adopted, Guzman feels she has "empowered teachers to think outside the box when it comes to teaching math and science; I support them as they take baby steps and pretty soon the door flies open and they soar."

Joe Todd, secondary technology integration coach in GCISD, first opted to work in education because of great experiences with his teachers. He was particularly fond of his science teachers: "I would help them with things before school. I was in AP biology and had a new teacher who let us do innovative experiments and that really hooked me into science." People around Todd noticed his skills as an effective communicator; his parents were both in the medical field and their conversations with him were rich in science. One of his aspirations was to work with adult learners and collaborate in ways to work together.

While working as a middle school science teacher and department chair, he was encouraged to become a district science coach. He saw a need for teachers to be better at instructing and engaging students and to get them into the hands-on part of teaching. According to Todd, "my goals were to build capacity in educators and broaden the reach and impact of the program within my district." He had a rich skill set in organization and program development and hammering out the details with teachers:

> Beyond working with a district, I had a unique opportunity to work with a company that developed curriculum and technology for science education. I was able to see many fascinating ways to quantify natural phenomenon and what a digital environment for education can look like. Within the company I had the opportunity to help districts to take their standards or the NGSS standards and think through how they would align the use of sensors and apparatus to master new standards. I identified gaps in technology usage to address their new standards.

Todd's career has now returned him to the public school setting where he is using his background in technology to work as a technology integration coach on secondary campuses. Joe is an advocate for STEM practices and an experienced coach; he finds his experiences to be major factors in the success he has had as a coach and the way he addresses his role.

5

The STEM Coach Job Description

Work Days: 191

School District HR Online posting for a STEM coaching position:
The Program Support Specialist (STEM) is a master teacher who serves in the capacity of a site-based content coach and comprehensive reform design coach, and continuously provides leadership and expertise at the local school level to support improvement in teacher instruction. This position reports to the School Principal and/or Associate Superintendent based on their assigned location and is on a year-to-year appointment.

Position: STEM Program Specialist, Certified

Duties and Responsibilities:
◆ Promotes district instructional priorities by providing support and demonstration of the following skills: training-modeling coaching: instructional guidance necessary for the operation of the STEM-based instructional program.
◆ Ensures fidelity of implementation of the site based comprehensive reform model via monitoring and observation. Conducts informal classroom observations and provides feedback to teachers and assists with the development of new teachers.
◆ Facilitates professional learning communities and assists teachers with collaborative lesson planning.

◆ Monitors students' progress and arranges for academic interventions based on formative and summative assessments.
◆ Conducts analysis of formative and summative student data and recommends modifications to instruction.
◆ Uses observation and achievement data to identify professional development needs and designs and delivers site based professional learning.
◆ Assists with reviewing classroom lesson plans and provides lesson plan feedback to teachers with a STEM focus.
◆ Serves as a facilitator to engage parents in gaining a level of exposure and understanding as it relates to the comprehensive reform model.
◆ Other duties as assigned.

Requirements
CERTIFICATION:
Must possess a valid teacher certificate.

EDUCATION:
Bachelor's degree required.

EXPERIENCE:
Minimum of three years of teacher experience required. STEM experience required.

Reports to: Principal

Are you ready to apply? Feel like you are qualified? The above job description is straight forward, comprehensive, and yet open-ended. It does state the candidate needs to have proficiency as a master teacher in their content area, and have the capacity to coach in the content area as well as in the practices of STEM-based instruction.

As we noted previously, STEM is about building capacity in teachers to think more deeply about the content of their lessons and to use effective strategies for delivery of the content for understanding and mastery of the content standards. Do you have the skills for helping teachers to view their content through the lens of STEM interdisciplinary instruction, as well as being held accountable for student achievement gains? Are you able emotionally to commit to carefully coach a teacher into thinking more deeply about their practice and to use more effective instructional strategies? This requires a high-quality coaching protocol in which you are well practiced. What is your level of expertise in coaching? Do you need to learn a bit more about that, or have you already received quality training in coaching? If you can say yes, then read on!

Did you pay attention to the requirement for being a reform-design coach? Did you know that includes an understanding of how to create a compelling and urgent need in teachers to inspect their thinking, philosophy, and beliefs about their instructional practices and student engagement? Are you aware of the extensive body of research about change and how difficult it is to transition to a constructivist mindset once a behaviorist mindset is part of the school culture? Have you thought about how you will work to change the ingrained patterns of behavior that are based in the core belief systems of teachers?

Before you change your career goals and decide that perhaps coaching is not your niche, these topics are discussed in the portion of this chapter called Roles and responsibilities of a STEM coach. In Part II, we share the ways master STEM specialists use coaching as a vehicle for the transformation of a traditional campus into one that embraces and grows the capacity for students to discover and solve problems using a STEM-based learning environment. Finally, in Parts III and IV, we focus on ways to help campuses transition to a STEM-based program by taking steps to create a student-centered, inquiry-based learning environment in classrooms and on campus.

The transformation of a campus to a STEM-based learning community involves stakeholders and events that inform and involve the community. With growth towards role-model status, high-caliber teaching and learning occur within the organization. A STEM-based organization breaks down content silos, uses learning based on student engagement, interdisciplinary studies, innovative thinking, designing solutions, authentic issues, and a deep understanding of the interconnectedness of science, mathematics, ELA, social studies, and the fine arts.

Roles and Responsibilities of a STEM Coach

The primary role of an instructional coach is to be a resource to campus leadership—the principal and leadership team—in meeting the goals of the district. The goals are usually summarized in the Campus Improvement Plan. Although principals are the instructional leader of their campuses, they enlist the support of coaches and instructional specialists to work specifically with teachers through professional development, mentoring, and coaching to improve teacher instruction. In turn, if done effectively student achievement will improve as result of high-quality instruction.

The purpose of the STEM coach compared to that of a content instructional specialist is to focus on changing the traditional ways of teaching and assessing content knowledge to more effective and engaging instructional practices that will increase the likelihood that students will go into STEM fields upon graduation. Often a STEM coach has a dual role of being the thought leader for the campus in ways to integrate STEM-based practices, but to also be a content area instructional specialist/coach, typically in science, math, technology, or all three.

Instructional specialists are typically focused on helping teachers become more skillful in the craft knowledge of a specific content area by using highly effective and content-specific instructional strategies, guiding the development of assessments, interpreting assessment data, and organizing resources for the content area teachers. Little integration, cross-disciplinary conversations, or use of the themes and skills from other content are incorporated into instruction or student work. Following the traditional approach that has been in place since schools began focusing on the 3Rs; each R is being taught and studied as a separate subject. Subjects are locked into content silos that are centered on content-specific methods and models of teaching and knowing.

STEM coaching is also based on content knowledge, content-specific skills, and student mastery of content standards. But, it is also an innovative approach to blending content learning, engaging in STEM-based integrated problem-solving, and using critical thinking. Instructional coaches can be STEM-based instructional coaches, still using their content-specific perspectives, but viewing it through the lens of STEM. Focusing on STEM instructional strategies and behaviors brings a real-world, authentic view to learning and student work. A good STEM coach can walk the fine line between challenging the status quo of teaching content in isolation and bringing change to a change-weary faculty

A reading teacher using a content lens may follow this scenario. In an English Language Arts classroom reading is frequently taught through reading literature or the fictional accounts of characters engaged in an event or situation. The reading-based study focuses on comprehension of the text, character development, the plot, buildup, climax and resolution of the situation, and identification and definitions of the vocabulary words found in the text.

A reading class taught by an ELA teacher through a STEM lens may include reading primary documents or non-fiction text written by a person engaged in an inquiry about a real-world situation. The STEM-based lesson focuses on the environment of the situation—the science, math, and social studies factors influencing the situation. The teacher then invites the students to determine the problem, the criteria, and constraints imposed by the environment. By dividing them into design teams the teacher asks them to become creative and design several possible solutions. In each case, reading skills are utilized and learned, but the first scenario is based on a siloed approach, whereas the second is STEM-based.

The goals and responsibilities of coaching through STEM are to move all content and elective teachers forward; taking steps (even baby steps) in adopting STEM instructional models and strategies. Coaching content-specific teachers through STEM means building in them the capacity to adapt their former content-specific strategies and adopt new STEM-based ones. STEM coaching means supporting teachers as they develop new ways of thinking about engaging students in high-quality work for the success of all the students. Coaching through STEM is the picture postcard of students mastering content objectives while being learning partners with their teacher in authentic, collaborative, inquiry-based, interdisciplinary, skill-rich experiences.

Joe Ferrara was a science instructional coach in Dallas-Ft Worth ISD's Instructional Team. According to Ferrara, "In Ft. Worth ISD their Curriculum and Instruction departments were separate." As members of Instruction, the coaches were under the Leadership Group who drove the instructional and academic focus for their region of the district. That gave Ferrara, as the only secondary science instructional coach, an opportunity to have facetime with campus leadership—the principals. He used that time to make sure that whatever he did in their building was in line with their priorities and initiatives.

Every campus had a Campus Improvement Plan (CIP) and as the science instructional coach he would review each campus's CIP with the principal, focusing on the instructional plan for science. That gave Ferrara an opportunity to learn about each campus principal's instructional focus, goals, and data. By checking in with the principals when on their campus there was open communication to discuss the links and disconnects between what he saw happening in classrooms and what they wanted in support of their goals. The principals saw coaches as resources in meeting the goals of their plans. Ferrara was then able to schedule time to coach with specific teachers, with the backing of the campus principal. Their goals were the same, and Ferrara's role as a coach was clearly defined.

Responsibilities and Roles Outside of Coaching

In some districts, campus STEM coaches find themselves as an extension of district administration. Sara Jones, a science curriculum and instructional coach with the Harmony Schools in Houston, finds her role places her technically on the administration team. One of her other duties outside of her science curriculum and instructional coaching role and providing PD is to conduct mock observations of all science teachers for the nine campuses she is assigned. This requires the same 40 hours of training that principals receive, plus quarterly calibration trainings. Jones spends a large portion of the first semester using the new scoring system for these teacher observations, which replaced the professional development assessment system (PDAS). By conducting observations that do not count toward teacher formal evaluations, she is able to show teachers how the new scoring system will hold them accountable for their instructional practices.

According to Jones, "I score like a principal but it doesn't count towards their formal evaluation. By helping teachers understand how they will be evaluated helps me to support them in improving their practice by focusing on the skills from the evaluation system." The evaluation is divided into domains and the mock observation gives her data for coaching.

As coach, Jones spends much of her time working with teachers on classroom management strategies. She has found that many middle school teachers struggle with classroom management and those struggles get in the way of great instruction, especially project-based learning (PBL). PBL is more unstructured and student-led. In addition, she supports teachers in STEM integration through Harmony's PBL model, writes professional development, and works with the curriculum team to create pacing calendars, lesson planning unit guides, and warm-ups from the released test items. Sara also plans and runs a Houston Harmony middle school science fair, meets with administrators to report the trends she notices through data from testing and her observations, and creates and implements plans to improve instruction for struggling teachers.

Jodi Marchesso, in her role as the STEM science instructional specialist in Pasadena USD, provides support to other district programs. She works in the Instruction program but works with the Curriculum program as well. It was at her sole discretion to select a STEM-based curriculum and resources for adoption in science. She is responsible for the district-wide Innovation Exposition, which is Pasadena USD's version of a science fair, coordinates with community partners, and is part of a district-wide decision-making team.

Recently in my office we had a discussion about being more of a curriculum specialist or an instructional coach; some can see it as two very separate entities, I think they are intertwined. We need to understand the curriculum but to push it forward and I need to work with teachers very closely as they choose the instructional practices they will use with their students.

Marchesso's district has a number of specialized programs such as a dual language program offered in Spanish and Mandarin, STEM schools K-8, and College and Career Pathways Magnet Schools. So, another one of her responsibilities outside of her role as a STEM instructional coach is to spend a lot of time in coaching meetings to guide the capacity of the campus coaches: "Campus coaches are the onsite coaches and I act in an advisory role during these meetings." In the middle of the year, the focus shifts to sustainability, when the STEM grant funds and the coaching roles go away. Marchesso states, "We are building capacity in our coaches to help teachers as support rather than to run their campus programs."

Through coaching and facilitating, she has implemented the pathway for so much growth! Her long-range plans are for a four- to five-year rollout for the Next Generation Science Standards (NGSS). This requires the background work and assessment planning for making it work as an integrated model. Marchesso's year-long plan began with conversations with the campus coaches to build a common understanding of STEM and NGSS integration. She also wanted to strengthen their leadership capacity. By the middle of the year the middle school campus coaches were writing integrated curriculum and assessments, and using their leadership skills in planning at the campus level with teachers. As her plan came to an end at the close of the school year, the middle school campus coaches were moving from being the STEM leaders on each campus to becoming facilitators in planning. They will work with teachers for STEM and NGSS integrated lessons and their implementation in classrooms.

The Unwritten Roles and Other Duties as Assigned

As part of the campus, each faculty member can be called on to fill in for emergency situations, such as fire drills, assemblies, and other large events. Within their roles as district-deployed, campus-based coaches they may be asked to step into classrooms for times when testing is going on and students need separate administration of tests. On the whole, it is important for campus leadership to honor the role of the coach and instructional specialists whose tasks are large and schedules are filled with preparing for coaching sessions, observations, data analysis, and providing training for the campus.

Dr. Leslie Hancock, as an onsite instructional coach who works to support STEM, says she also helps teachers to apply for grants, provides training at department instructional focus meetings, as well as delivering onsite professional development in areas such as advancement via individual determination (AVID) strategies, white boards, and dyslexia simulations. She states:

> I entered into the role knowing it was nebulous and this was my opportunity to define the role for my campus and myself. There were few expectations except to work hard and to serve the people of my campus. I was tasked to follow the lead of my leadership.

Hancock helps with data analysis for assessments that are embedded, curriculum-based, and state standardized. Data analysis can be time consuming, but with her background in number crunching in Evaluation Services at Baylor University, data analysis is manageable, if not enjoyable.

How Much Teaching Experience Should a STEM Coach Have?

Kristi Adams, former STEM coach with K20 in Oklahoma, relayed a recent conversation she had with an elementary teacher in one of her pre-service education sessions. Do you agree with the advice she gave? As Adams told me, the teacher was young and new in elementary education and teaching. She approached Adams and said that she wanted to become a STEM coach. Adams' advice was meted out carefully but this is what she said,

> Eventually you will be a wonderful coach—but you need experience in the classroom. You need five years at least, working with students using inquiry-based strategies, trying new things, using your imagination, and allowing students to take the reins. You will need to discover how students view the world and how they process math and science. You need to know how to reach students and not just teach them. Take the time to work with teachers who know how to reach students. Get a master's in a field of math or science to increase your knowledge so you can be a resource to the people you want to coach.

Dillon Chevalier was a highly effective third-year teacher when he was promoted to STEM coach in the Harmony Public Schools in Dallas. He chose to approach coaching science teachers from a position of both a listener and a learner. Many teachers were older and had more experience than him. Treating them as the experts and not challenging them about their content worked for him as a coach. The teachers had ownership of the content; they knew it best. Chevalier felt that this approach and his commitment to the teachers allowed them to be less apprehensive of a coaching session and it established a level of respect between the two of them. Some opened up immediately and saw him as a colleague and resource, but for others it took a while longer.

> Initially, I had the most trouble with only having three years of teaching experience and lacking some of the coaching skills such as how to communicate possible strategies effectively. I could tell them about district procedures or strategies that worked for me, but I wasn't sure how to help them solve certain problems specific to their situation. The teachers I worked with had great personalities and the drive was there, but because I didn't have a lot of the tools and skills coaches need, I wasn't yet comfortable sharing ideas or modeling instructional practices for them.

To become a STEM consultant, Janelle McLaughlin did not receive any additional training. She learned as she went along, drawing on past experiences as a teacher and administrator. "I learned from my mistakes and successes. I attended many professional development trainings as a teacher and as a curriculum director, so I am able to draw from all of those." McLaughlin stated, "My mistakes and first steps help me to learn." She partnered with those she considered to be really good coaches, who mentored her, shared resources, and encouraged her to ask many questions.

Dr. Ferrara at UT Dallas has a background in biology. He received his alternative certification in education after serving as an electronics-engineering technician in the Air Force and as a tech in the transplant immunology lab at Southwestern Medical Center in Dallas, TX. Ferrara's career in education took him from the middle school and high school classrooms, to being an instructional coach at the secondary level. Although not having an extensive background in a university-based pre-service program, Ferrara used his experiences from being in the Air Force, working at the Medical Center lab, and being a successful science teacher and department chair to be able to assist science teachers and administrators as a resource and partner in their students' success.

The actual impact you have as a coach comes from your credibility as a teacher and a leader. When you ask teachers to step out and take risks by changing their instructional philosophy and practice, they need to know you have been in their shoes and experienced the same things. Teachers need to know you have experiences that include failing, making mistakes, receiving and using feedback, and finding other ways to try to make it work. Teachers and administrators will accept the gentle pressure you are applying for their movement in changing their practice when they know your support is genuine and sincere.

A credible coach understands the needs of an adult learner compared to those of a student in a classroom. The coach, with a well-stocked toolkit of instructional strategies that works with students in the classroom and another that works with adults, provides a platform for addressing the changes you would like to help them attain. When teachers are treated with respect because of their experiences and know you have enough experience to appreciate their struggles, you will gain their trust. A depth of content knowledge and well-polished skills in the practices of your content allows you as a coach to speak from experience and help you to be seen as a resource, as someone who will be able to not only tell them the "what" but also be able to explain the "why."

Coaches who have experience participate in conferences as presenters. They are conference participants and are able to network within the STEM education community for an exchange of ideas about best practices in all areas of STEM education. Coaches are comfortable in speaking with campus leadership about the needs of the teachers they coach. They work in partnership with campus leaders to find ways to fund scholarships, awards, partnerships, etc., as a means of providing resources to meet the teachers' needs.

These skills come from study, observations, experiences in teaching, and an awareness of the respect a coach holds in an educational community. It is not for the faint of heart, but it is extremely rewarding and worthwhile when you enter into the field of coaching with an understanding of the skills, knowledge, and experiences needed to be credible and the willingness to continue to work on your craft through continued training, research, and feedback.

How Much Does a STEM Coach Need to Know About Coaching?

Marisa Guzman did not receive formal training for leadership or coaching, prior to accepting the position as a math–science STEM instructional coach. The majority of her training was content or curriculum based. To close that gap in her skill set as a coach she meets with the instructional team of district coaches every other Friday for a training day. The district coaches learn about the strategies they are to share with teachers. The sessions are more like "train the trainer" sessions for the instructional strategies to be used by teachers, rather than strategies to be used by the coaches for coaching. That is learned through personal reading, personal experiences, and by attending professional conferences and workshops.

Guzman's principal finds it amusing that Guzman never requests to go to conferences. The teachers on her campus value the PD that conferences provide and request to attend. To save funds, the principal usually suggests that Guzman attends and brings back the information to the teachers. But Guzman speaks up for the teachers' requests because she values the common learning experiences they share as a team. Usually, the discussion ends with the teachers receiving permission to attend as a team and Guzman goes as well. The benefit of that arrangement is that through the common learning experiences they have background knowledge to further investigate their new understandings as a team back on their campus.

According to Joe Ferrara, now director of the UT Dallas Institute for Instructional Excellence, "When I first was hired to be an instructional coach in Ft Worth ISD, I hoped my role as a coach would look differently than what I experienced as a teacher." The experience he mentioned was when a coach came in and sat in his classroom for 30 minutes and observed him, then left with no conversation or feedback. He says, "I felt inadequate and developed a stigma towards coaches."

Ferrara had an opportunity to attend professional development on Cognitive Coaching as part of his training as an instructional specialist with Dallas-Ft Worth ISD and he began to develop his approach to coaching. He also looked at different instructional coaching models including Jim Knight's Instructional Coaching model. In his opinion, Knight's model was a dynamic approach to instructional coaching built on seven Partnership Principles and really allowed him to become more comfortable in his role as a coach.

Kyndra Johnson, the director of STEM Education and Curriculum Innovation in Lancaster ISD, an all-STEM district, started as a science instructional coach in Dallas ISD. It was a new position for Dallas ISD as a teacher leader out of the classroom:

> I learned to be an instructional coach through the Institute for Learning. We learned about "Accountable Talk" and developed a deep understanding of high quality, rigorous teaching and learning. It was my role and responsibility to help teachers ensure each student was having access to quality instruction.

Johnson also attended training through the Regional Education Service Center, presented by Jim Knight. His program influenced her to use a sound-coaching model as she was working to help teachers to reflect on their instructional practices. Another valuable training course that Johnson attended was at an ASCD conference. Through their sessions Johnson learned more about coaching with teachers as an effort to increase the depth of their content knowledge and the quality of their instructional practices. It reinforced for her the value of strong relationships. Research shared with the attendees showed how a coaching model could be effective in support of growing teachers in their pedagogy and content.

The research focus proved to her that PD followed by instructional coaching is more effective than PD alone. According to Johnson, "Those experiences proved to me that if a district is going to increase student achievement by taking teachers from where they are to where our students needed them to be, using instructional coaching would be the most effective professional development model."

Which STEM Practices Should a STEM Coach Know?

An effective STEM-based teacher or STEM coach needs to develop an understanding of the ultimate impact of a STEM philosophy on the student success. For teachers, it is their philosophy that drives the STEM focus which includes the ability to break down the silos of separate content areas during instruction and to use authentic practices of those engaged in that study in the world outside the classroom; as scientists, engineers, authors, mechanics, business people, as well as those in construction, education, service industry, etc. This should be based on the 21st Century Skills supported by the workforce and the requirements for college and career readiness established by each state.

The adult world outside of school is driven by daily problems and situations that need solutions. The ability to recognize situations that are problems that require solutions, to identify the constraints within the problem, and to be able to articulate the criterion that defines a successful solution are abilities required for a person to survive in the real world. Every day, within our classrooms, STEM students should be engaged in creative and critical thinking processes at an age-appropriate level, dealing with challenging and authentic problems. Development of these skills happens only when students are intrigued by the problem and tenacious in their drive to develop a creative solution.

A novice STEM teacher, working with an effective coach, will gain skills to guide students in asking questions to clarify the issues, to plan with collaborative teams to develop a process or prototype that can begin to work towards a solution. Using engineering design challenges, PBLs, and other hands-on investigations are the beginning of this journey. Eventually teachers will develop their own routines and protocols for addressing these types of STEM-based strategies.

Mindset is a way of being either open or closed to accepting a challenge and the ability to accept failure either as a step in moving forward or as a roadblock blocking further progress. Students with open mindsets can work with some lack of specificity in working through problems, and are open to constructivism and inquiry-based learning opportunities. Students with closed mindsets struggle with not knowing the criteria and constraints upfront because if they don't know the solution immediately they do not want to risk finding the solution through trial and error.

It is important for students in a STEM-based classroom to deal with confounding issues at age-appropriate levels; to be able to develop the persistence to persevere when the solution is not quick, easy, or forthcoming. It is hard to teach and equally hard to adopt. Teachers need to design situations that allow students to fail, make mistakes, receive and use feedback, and persevere in finding other ways to try to make it work. They will learn to work at shaping their own work ethics and philosophies for dealing with such situations in the real world.

STEM teachers will develop fluency in their abilities to select instructional resources or construct experiences that support an inquiry-based, student-centered, STEM-focused classroom. A coach needs to become knowledgeable of the STEM-based programs and supports provided by the community and universities in the area. It is of additional value for the STEM coach to have a firm grasp of the needs of the workforce and the trends in employment in STEM and non-STEM fields in their area and nationally.

The Texarkana school district set into policy the requirement for STEM teachers to complete two graduate-level STEM courses prior to entering a STEM classroom. The teachers were also required to complete a master's degree in Curriculum and Instruction while employed as STEM teachers. Elementary STEM teachers were required to obtain state certification in Master Mathematics Teaching (MMT). The district decided to join with a university-based STEM program to accomplish two important things:

1. A common understanding of being STEM-centered with highly developed skills in the implementation of STEM instructional strategies through earning certification in STEM
2. An understanding and expertise in STEM content for rigorous and accelerated cross-curricular instruction.

Most district science supervisors and coordinators are becoming the STEM leaders in their districts. STEM-based professional development is required for any leader to understand the transition. Sharry Whitney, in Lewisville ISD, honed her skills as a professional developer, by first gaining her master's degree in Administration and learning how to facilitate professional development at all levels. Whitney passionately wanted to lead teachers in their desire to grow and improve their craft knowledge. She focused on learning more about inquiry-based practices and how to incorporate STEM and 21st Century Skills into science-based instruction.

> As a science supervisor I was in every secondary science classroom in our district of over 50,000 students, and saw that the teachers' issues and struggles were very similar—not enough time, not enough budget, and not enough support. I needed to find ways to help them to continue to grow in their profession so they could meet the needs of their students. Getting my degree opened my perspective, provided a springboard for many creative ways to address these issues, and made many resources available for me to use in my role.

The integration of math, science, technology, and problem-solving is fundamental for Denise Fisher, former STEM coordinator and K-12 STEM coach in Texarkana ISD:

> In the beginning of my teaching career my first love was science. Because of that, I have a master's degree in science education. As classroom technology became more widely used in schools, I found it to be a way for my students to more fully integrate math with science. As we worked with graphs and data, I found they would back away from the higher levels of thinking required for the integration of math concepts and solving problems. I knew that this reaction was typical of most MS students and that is where kids fall down in their preparation for STEM coursework for college.

Fisher personally wanted a deeper understanding of how to teach these math–science concepts to her students so they would understand and be successful. So, she went back to college to get a master's degree and certification in Mathematics Education. For her, that's when it all came together. She passionately thinks students need STEM for their futures.

Fisher feels strongly that STEM made it happen for her students. Texarkana ISD graduates are being accepted and graduating with STEM degrees from Ivy League colleges in numbers never seen before. For Fisher, this is evidence of the success of their K-12 STEM pipeline. When students leave the STEM program they are college and career ready. They are proud of the STEM endorsement on their diplomas as proof that they are prepared.

According to Fisher, to have instructional skills to teach in an integrated STEM program, teachers must be content experts in what they teach.

Training in instructional strategies and having a growth mindset to learn with and for the students are at the heart of a successful STEM program:

> The additional certification made the difference but it is hard to ask every teacher to get a master's degree in STEM—even if they teach kindergarten. But, as our STEM program was being designed I asked, 'what do we need to do to prepare the teachers for STEM?' Based on the required depth of knowledge and instructional skills, the decision was made to require a greater level of preparation and STEM certification. Most teachers chose to move forward with the additional coursework. To keep their skills sharp and the passion for continued learning alive, we supported them during the school year through professional development, coaching, and professional learning communities (PLC).

Lancaster ISD has invested in its STEM teachers. Lancaster ISD shares the investment of covering tuition costs for teachers in the program with funds from their STEM grant award from Texas Instruments. District leaders can see the benefits of growing STEM teachers through a university STEM program. The district planned for all 6–12 grade math and science teachers to attend the University of North Texas (UNT) to get their master's degree in STEM. During the 2015–2016 school year 18 had completed their degrees, with a planned total of 40. The program is sustainable through the community investing in its teachers by contributing to the Texas Instrument Foundation.

STEM teachers receive specific coach support and PD to assist them in using high-quality instructional practices and strategies as they nurture students through authentic, real-world, problem-solving scenarios and engineering design challenges. These are the added bonus of using a STEM lens in designing instruction for students of the next generation of critical thinkers and problem solvers.

During Joe Ferrara's time as a teacher he attended many professional development venues and realized each PD was not as practical as he had hoped. There usually was very little he could immediately take back to the classroom and use. Professional development was often a mix of theory and practice; he stated that rarely was time provided during the session to reflect on what that practice looked like in his classroom. As an instructional coach, he began to put together his ideas about science instruction from training he attended by Lynn Erickson, author of *Stirring The Head, Heart, And Soul: Redefining Curriculum, Instruction, And Concept-Based Learning* (2008). He began to connect his experiences—in the classroom, in industry, and as an administrator—into effective ways to train teachers in the use of a concept-based curriculum. To provide focus to coaching sessions, he developed operational language that he always used with teachers when discussing instruction. This resulted in shared understanding of his approach and increased substantive conversation during his sessions. He also promoted reflection and application time, providing teachers space to apply what they had learned to their classrooms. Instructional needs vary teacher by teacher and this time allows teachers to direct instruction towards student achievement.

6

How STEM Coaches Support
STEM Campuses

State-Level STEM Coaches

States such as Oklahoma, North Carolina, Iowa, Ohio, Kansas, and Texas have worked to disseminate and adopt effective STEM instructional practices statewide that include authentic hands-on learning to increase student engagement and achievement. National organizations such as STEMx Network are online networks of state STEM programs willing to share their STEM-based resources and hold conferences for networking. Some grants are available to bring high-quality STEM content and experiences to students from low-income, high-need schools. Many programs support teachers' growth in STEM programs and others support innovative technologies that are intended to personalize student learning.

One focus for STEM funding in Texas, and similarly in several other states, was the development of the Texas Science, Technology, Engineering, and Mathematics (T-STEM) Initiative. According to its website, Educate Texas is an organization used by the Texas Education Agency (TEA) to oversee the T-STEM program:

> Educate Texas provides a foundational approach to empower teachers, inspire students, and advance the studies in these four fields. The public–private initiative of academies, professional development centers and networks is designed to improve instruction and academic performance in science and mathematics-related subjects at secondary schools.

One of the ways Educate Texas supports the T-STEM initiative is to provide STEM coaches for the T-STEM academies that have applied for STEM-designation through the Texas Education Agency (TEA). Dr. Jennifer Stotts is a STEM education consultant and T-STEM coach with Educate Texas. Her background is rich and deep in instructional leadership. In her role as a T-STEM coach Stotts aims to move campuses forward in meeting T-STEM objectives as outlined in the *T-STEM Academies Design Blueprint* (2015) by working with district administrators.

The *T-STEM Academies Design Blueprint* provides a growth metric for determining where schools are in their transition from being traditional to being STEM-based. There are seven benchmarks in the T-STEM Blueprint:

1. Mission-Driven Leadership
2. T-STEM Culture
3. Student Outreach, Recruitment, and Retention
4. Teacher Selection, Development, and Retention
5. Curriculum, Instruction, and Assessment
6. Strategic Alliances
7. Academy Advancement and Sustainability (Educate Texas, 2015)

According to Stotts, "the cornerstone of the T-STEM academy learning is student engagement and exposure to innovation and design in STEM-focused instruction and learning that models real-world contexts."

Stotts meets regularly with secondary T-STEM designated academies and works in partnership with campus administrators, principals, and campus leaders who are accountable for the academic achievement of all students. This partnership allows each T-STEM academy and the TEA to accomplish their goals as they bring high-quality academics and STEM to the classroom. Although she does not specifically coach teachers, Stotts does observe in classrooms for instructional practices that incorporate the qualities of the T-STEM Blueprint.

The areas a T-STEM designated campus needs to improve upon are identified by analysis of several sets of data: teacher self-assessments, principal observations, and Stotts' observations. The data are collected and analyzed based on the criteria for each benchmark in the *T-STEM Academies Design Blueprint*. The areas in need of improvement are addressed in the campus improvement plan (CIP). The CIP includes a plan for teacher professional development, resources, and ways to make connections to the STEM world outside of the school campus in order to meet the benchmark criteria in the T-STEM Blueprint. Although project-based learning (PBL) is a big part of STEM and is considered non-negotiable, being STEM it is not just about PBL.

It is about the instructional strategies teachers use to get students engaged and interested in all things STEM: from classroom experiences, extracurricular activities, robotics, advanced academics, and Future City, to how students see themselves in future careers. It is not just about doing the STEM program requirements; it is about having a STEM mindset. Stotts states:

> That is my role. It is the role of the STEM coach to help schools see beyond obstacles and then to turn that visioning into action items that transform obstacles into steppingstones for success. STEM coaches apply that gentle pressure that promotes others to see beyond current realities, envision new possibilities, and then implement actions to measure change through the Blueprint—thus moving STEM forward for students, campus leaders, and teachers.

In Oklahoma, the K20 Center at the University of Oklahoma provides support to pre-K through sixth grade level teachers in the STEM content and pedagogy aligned to the College, Career, and Citizen (C3) curriculum developed by its program. Completion of the program prepares selected Oklahoma schools "by providing year-long professional development with regular onsite teacher visits and instructional materials for the classrooms." According to the K20 website, it is funded by the Oklahoma State Department of Education.

Kristi Adams, former K20 STEM coach but now a STEM consultant with St. Gregory's University, focused on outreach to public schools. Unlike the role of Dr. Stotts, Adams' role in the state-funded program was in coaching and providing three outreach PD sessions to teachers, built around the needs of the school. Each PD session centered on STEM pedagogy, content, or combination of both and lasted about three hours. The participants were from all content areas and all grade levels from pre-K to 12th grade. Teachers in the sessions learn, practice, and discuss implementation of strategies that are important to the development of STEM instructional skills and student achievement. The PD sessions showcase the use of the 5E lesson model and inquiry-based practices.

For Adams, coaching was the next step towards increasing teacher implementation and was set up on an individual basis. If teachers in the sessions indicated they need support along the way, the K20 STEM coach set up one-to-one or group sessions to work with them. Often ideas were shared through Google docs so they were collaborative and could be discussed online.

Adams feels that, "STEM is about integrating curriculum that builds on the natural curiosity of students. So content is integrated within STEM, and students are not just studying one content area or just plugging and chugging equations; it is about thinking about a problem and making connections to the real world where integration is the way it is." Adams believes:

> Students should learn how to investigate their own questions within a specific content area. Content specific teachers feel the accountability in what they are to teach and limit the focus of questions. STEM gives teachers and students the freedom to investigate their own questions as part of a broader question that accomplishes mastery of the content and brings in STEM skills and content areas to make a real-world connection. Using Driving Questions that are broad and intriguing, can be a great strategy for the STEM-centered teacher.

The K20 project recruits K-12 campuses into the STEM program. St. Gregory University, where Adams is a STEM coach, provides outreach that begins with two-week summer institutes for STEM pedagogy and content foundations for the program. The combined university outreach program—campus-based professional development, coaching, and resources provided for the campus and teachers—helps teachers to make the transition from a traditional campus to a STEM learning environment.

STEM coaches from university-based STEM centers provided support to campuses at the state level. Felecia Pittman's role at the UT Dallas T-STEM Center was to serve as a STEM coach to campus leadership and teachers. Sitting down with the campus leader and the leadership team, she provided them an opportunity to draw up an action plan based on the *T-STEM Academies Design Blueprint*. Frequent visits included time to reflect on where the campus was in implementation, on roadblocks, and how to make greater strides towards becoming a role model STEM academy.

As the T-STEM Center coach, Pittman provided PD for all the teachers on the campus in STEM strategies and had an opportunity to participate in classroom coaching as well. "My PD and classroom coaching was based upon implementing PBLs and watching as teachers worked through the components."

Pittman, in her role as an Educate Texas leadership coach, worked in supporting teachers as well, but that depended on the campus. On the campuses where she was invited to meet with teachers and to sit in on classroom instruction, she enjoyed providing feedback afterwards. It was an extension of what she did when she coached teachers at UT Dallas as a T-STEM coach. The principal walked with her as she observed classrooms, and was able to provide information about the teachers, their expertise, background, and areas where they needed support.

After observing a PBL, Pittman would use a protocol for guiding their reflection on how it worked, she provided feedback, and then they planned for the next steps. If Pittman saw that several teachers on the same campus were having the same difficulties, she would schedule a PLC to work through the stumbling blocks. As a group they would generate ideas for another way to tackle the problem.

District-Level STEM Coaches

Coaches deployed at the district level provide a broad range of services to campus leadership in supporting implementation of district initiatives. From the district level, there are many ways principals, campus leaders, and teachers can be supported. Often it is through coaches that the implementation of STEM strategies with teachers most often happens. This section provides a sampling of the many ways districts utilize STEM coaches who are centrally deployed.

Lancaster ISD is a Texas Education Agency T-STEM designated district in northeast Texas. The community stakeholders worked with the district to embrace and promote STEM in the school district. All parties saw the benefits that changing the instructional focus of the school district to a STEM focus would do to enhance the success of the economy and industry of the area. The district's superintendent and administration team reorganized the academic support structures in the district to embrace and enhance this new vision.

The STEM and Curriculum Innovation division was reorganized to provide support to teachers and campuses. Kyndra Johnson was named Director of STEM Education and Curriculum Innovation. Her role as director was to work with and support each principal as the primary instructional leader of his or her campus: "At first we didn't have coaches and we did our best to be of service and support assessment and instruction. We were designing curriculum and assessments, and focused on PBLs which were both project-based and problem-based as a way to integrate STEM."

The Lancaster ISD curricular team consulted with the National Institute for Excellence in Teaching (NIET) and chose to use its teacher advancement program (TAP) as part of the solution to low achievement gains. Through the TAP program Lancaster coaches addressed depth of content knowledge and use of innovative instructional strategies by teachers for student academic growth. The trained instructional coaches utilized the TAP coaching strategies and PLCs for clusters of teacher learners.

They joined any STEM training they could find. They also attended the annual NSTA STEM Expo and the annual T-STEM Conference sponsored by Educate Texas. By attending professional development at the UT Dallas Center for STEM Education and Research (C-CER) they gained more ideas about PBLs and continued their learning through book studies about STEM. "We became acclimated to quality instructional practices and STEM strategies, which would be integral in providing our coaches with a rich background."

PBL coaches have evolved in Lancaster ISD and are now classified as STEM specialists. They have nine coaches and one coordinator. They are all master teachers that represent the core areas, but they have adopted a STEM literacy philosophy that infuses STEM across disciplines. The coaches work together but differently. The specialists are central-office deployed and are the curriculum designers; their roles are multi-faceted. They work on campuses supporting teachers with pedagogy and strategies while the central office team primarily is designing curriculum based in STEM. The curriculum has integrated math, science, and literacy as the instructional model. PBLs are understood as connections across the content in all aspects, even PE.

The instructional and STEM coaches focus on the district's academic achievement goals through high-quality instructional practices while integrating the 21st Century Skills associated with STEM. Based on the data gathered by Johnson, each campus's needs are different and the coaches use data to design the targeted supports that are offered. District coaches provide both developmentally adjusted coaching and professional development:

> We are making gains as each year we get better and are providing many learning opportunities through PLCs and professional development. Each has a place in moving our district further head in STEM. We are focused on service, having an open mindset, and having a positive attitude about what we are trying to do in helping teachers achieve their goals.

According to Johnson, "I think quality instruction involves a diverse array of strategies and it demonstrates multiple modes of delivery. STEM has the flexibility to be creative and quality instruction has the creativity individualized. They are willing to take risks." Risk-taking is still being learned in her district. Teachers embrace PBL as a common way to find solutions. She believes quality instruction will emerge with students leading and stepping out of the box more frequently.

Denise Fisher, a founding STEM coordinator and K-12 STEM coach with the Texarkana ISD, worked with a cadre of master teachers who became the district's K-12 STEM coaches. Together they researched, studied, learned, and achieved a command of a deep knowledge base about STEM and STEM instructional practices. The cadre of master teachers, as K-12 STEM coaches, worked with administrators and teachers to support the transition of their traditional campuses to STEM campuses. To successfully use their extensive and strong foundation they found it was important to tie their campus coaching efforts to a university program that promoted STEM practices.

Dr. John Doughney of Grapevine-Colleyville ISD indicated that the master teachers followed an adapted *T-STEM Academies Design Blueprint* from Educate Texas 2010, for the development of the vision for their STEM campus at Cannon Elementary. Because Educate Texas does not provide STEM-designation to elementary campuses unless they are connected to a STEM-designated ninth grade program, it was necessary to adapt the secondary requirements to those appropriate for an elementary STEM program. Their principal utilized the district's STEM coach's support and a STEM consultant to develop their organizational framework. Cannon leadership focused on habits of mind and the authentic learning experiences that they wanted to provide for their students. As they mapped out their STEM vision and expectations, it was written to include a future pipeline so that all GCISD STEM campuses could apply the same organizational philosophy and *T-STEM Design Blueprint*.

In the GCISD STEM program, the directors of science, math, and career and technology education work specifically with the STEM initiatives. There is one STEM coach, who is part of a bigger district administrative team. The district-level STEM coach is responsible for the PD of STEM teachers and the guidance for development of new STEM academies. This district-level role was set up to guide and support the two STEM campuses: a whole campus elementary STEM model at Cannon and a STEM school-within-a-school middle school model at Grapevine Middle School. The STEM coach role is to assist the four directors in planning for the future development of a high school STEM academy. At the district level, the STEM coach also provides a safety net for student achievement and getting the work done.

In GCISD, there is one STEM technology integration specialist who is also part of a bigger team of district-level instructional coaches and liaisons. Although district-trained, all specialists, instructional coaches, and liaisons are campus-based. The STEM technology integration specialist supports the elementary and middle school STEM teachers for implementation of STEM-based technologies such as robotics, Arduino/circuit boards, etc. He provides support as they work through transitioning to the subtle differences required for STEM instruction. Although working with both STEM campuses, he reports to the STEM elementary principal.

The Curriculum and Instruction (C&I) Division in GCISD provides support to all campuses through a sophisticated instructional support model. The model is made up of division directors, campus liaisons, and instructional coaches. The development of this model was a result of a lack of district-wide instructional cohesion. The district could not guarantee delivery of an equitable instructional model. Instructional quality was not a mechanism that was guaranteed and did not happen on every campus every day. Through the C&I strategic plan put in place by LEAD 2021 and the development of this model for its implementation, cohesion for the C&I Division has been possible. Quality instruction throughout the district is the result.

Based on the model, the district chose to place learning liaisons on each campus. They became the learning liaisons between the campus and C&I. The liaisons report to both the principal and C&I. C&I executive director Doughney states: "This is the single most important part of our model; making a tremendous difference in cohesion of practice and guaranteed quality of instruction." Liaisons meet and train with C&I monthly so they have the same background and training. But, they go to the campus daily working only with teachers and not students. They keep the campus connected to the district's goals. The principals understand the importance of the campus-based liaisons and ensure the liaisons and coaches have the freedom and support to complete their tasks. Dr. Doughney provides oversight.

In the Lewisville ISD, STEM has begun to gain importance and as a result teachers are incorporating STEM activities into their classrooms through math, technology, and science. Sharry Whitney, as secondary science curriculum supervisor, recognized the importance of integrating math, science, and technology as the core of effective instruction and student learning. Having served at the district level as a science instructional coach and curriculum specialist, she worked mainly in the development of curriculum, assessments, data analysis, and data coaching with teachers. Whitney saw the value of technology-based initiatives, but also saw how they were separated from an integrated STEM focus. Campuses utilized technology-based lab simulations well, used tablets for reading and responding, and were able to do research that was Internet-based. They integrated technology for science lab activities but that was limited to using graphing calculators and science lab probe ware for measurements.

As science curriculum supervisor, Whitney's focus changed from working with teachers to working with administrators:

I became a servant leader. I served the principal's efforts to drive forward their campus initiatives, which included effective science instruction. I scheduled "walkthrough" observations of science classrooms with principals and assistant principals. I walked campuses each week with the secondary principals. We would sit down afterwards to discuss what we observed and their assessment of it. I felt fortunate to be able to walk each of the 25 campuses in our district two to three times a year.

Each principal had many ideas of what was needed to change the instructional practice of their science teachers. But, they always turned the question back to her and asked, "What do my teachers need?"

From her experience and background, Whitney knew inquiry in science was not honored or addressed in the science instruction her team observed. Her suggestion was that all teachers needed to understand and teach through inquiry and the principals agreed. Up until that point inquiry-based PD was offered in the summer and teachers could elect to attend. But from then on inquiry PD would be provided for all secondary science teachers during the school year and supported by principals. The principals provided administrative support and time for teachers to be out of the classroom for the three-day training. After a year, although trained, there was little implementation happening in the science classrooms.

Based on education research, Whitney knew that the principals themselves needed to see and learn what inquiry looked like. So, the next year the principals were trained in inquiry. Then, when Whitney walked with them, they observed for inquiry science. The principals supported their teachers as they were gaining skills in the inquiry strategies and practices. Principals also held teachers accountable for teaching through inquiry when they met with teachers to discuss their observations and conducted their annual evaluations.

According to Whitney, training campus administration was an eye-opening experience for them and gave them a true picture of what effective science instruction looks like:

> For true change in instructional practice to happen, teachers and principals need professional learning. In STEM-based science instruction it is imperative to hold teachers accountable for the nuances of good science instruction. They need to be knowledgeable. I have learned that when teachers get back to their campuses they are going to do what they think their principals want them to do. If the two forces don't have the same vision and work together, a positive change will not occur.

Pasadena USD serves students in Pasadena and Sierra Madre, CA. Jodi Marchesso is the STEM instructional coach working as a teacher on special assignment from within district administration. Under Marchesso's watch, the district's STEM learning culture is one that has been cultivated by the needs of its students. Among the general population there is a perception that does not come close to the reality of teaching in Pasadena USD. The old money is there, but 75% of the student population of the school district qualifies for federally provided funds for free and reduced-fee lunches. The economics of taxpayers living within the district's boundaries do not mirror the student population. It is a unique situation. There is a dichotomy within the educational system. Pasadena USD has the largest number of private schools and the largest number of group homes in the community.

The district has a number of specialized programs as well: dual-language schools that offer Spanish and Mandarin, STEM schools K-8, and College and Career Pathways Magnet Schools. The district administration works to provide for meeting the needs of its students by providing resources and supports based on the unique diversity of the students at each campus.

Marchesso's focus is to work with both new teachers and veteran teachers. Most of the science teachers are veterans averaging five years of teaching experience. There are many new teachers because of retirements based on a golden handshake option. Marchesso encounters resistance from both groups. Taking different approaches to coaching has proven effective in reducing some of it:

> If I work with them from a servant leader perspective—as an assistant during a lab, I can start to work on building trust. We can connect during PD days, but sometimes it can take a few years to get into a veteran teacher's classroom. After a PD training, it is easy for them to revert back to what was done before without coaching. When it gets tough they change back to their traditional teaching style.

There is a limit to what Marchesso is physically able to do in a week. K-8 teachers reach out usually because of content. The NGSS builds skills and knowledge by grade levels through sets of standards. She has focused on training K-5 teachers in the years prior to the NGSS adoption so they could start teaching to the new standards this school year.

> My focus this year is now on 6–12, especially MS and the integrated model in California, I focus on NGSS, how to read them, what they are, and how they are changing. I also work with new teachers. I support them in the beginning before the culture of the school gets to them. I try

to get them using good STEM and other instructional practice before the start of the school year.

Sara Jones is a science curriculum and instructional coach with Harmony Public Schools in the Houston Area. Harmony Schools are all over Texas so they are split into clusters that are equivalent to mini-districts. She is a cluster-level coach who works with kindergarten through eighth grade teachers at nine different campuses. Coaching is her primary role, since there are no campus-level coaches, but she still feels as though she doesn't get to work with teachers as often as she would prefer. Harmony has a high number of first-year teachers and international teachers, both of whom have greater needs. Splitting her time between so many campuses reduces the amount of time she can spend with these high-need teachers. Also, working with kindergarten through second grade teachers is difficult when teachers only teach science three days a week, and it may often get skipped to allow more time for reading and math.

Jones is responsible for district-wide professional development for all science teachers on the in-service day at the start of the year, and then four times during the school year on built-in PD days. For the nine campuses in her district, her PD plans include differentiation to meet the varied needs of the teachers she has observed and their need for differentiation strategies for their diverse learners.

> Based on my observations and mock evaluations there are several high yield STEM strategies to work on, and the 5E model is not well understood or implemented. Vocabulary development and close reading are also my focuses for using best practices for inquiry and literacy.

Harmony middle school students also must complete a project as part of Harmony's PBL program, so Jones spends some of her time planning, explanations, and giving PD on the program expectations and working with her middle school teachers to implement the program. Jones also plans and runs a cluster science fair for her middle schools. All of these duties outside of coaching take away time with teachers, which is one of the pitfalls of cluster/district coaching schemes.

Campus-Level STEM Coaches

The role of the campus principal is to implement district initiatives that are driven by expectations of the school board. These initiatives encompass goals for student achievement, lower dropout rates, accolades in extracurricular activities, maintaining a balanced budget, as well as the successful articulation of graduates into college and careers of merit. The responsibilities are large and challenging when the competing needs of management, building maintenance, transportation, and safety loom large.

As the instructional leader for their STEM campus, the additional role of ensuring that every classroom has a highly qualified and engaging teacher leading instruction is paramount. But, also the teacher must be engaged in the practices that forward their initiatives for engagement in STEM practices and skills. In order to ensure that consistent quality instruction is occurring on their campus, observations and evaluations are performed regularly, specifically looking for the teacher strategies and mindset that utilize the STEM practices and instructional strategies that are characteristic of STEM instruction.

When academic success is not being attained or STEM initiatives are not moving forward, funding may be provided to add campus instructional coaches, STEM integration coaches, department chairs, and specialists to the faculty. These roles are often used to move implementation of initiative-driven programs to effective levels. When the additional initiative is to integrate STEM into the culture and instructional focus of the campus, one of the added qualifications for the coach is to be well versed and practiced in STEM strategies and to have experience in its implementation.

In the Grapevine-Colleyville School District, under the direction of C&I executive director, Dr. John Doughney, the instructional coaches and liaisons serve all campuses including the STEM campuses but they coach from their perspective. By focusing on a generic but important question, "How do I improve this teacher's thinking?", they are able to cross content area boundaries to help teachers engage in deeper thinking. When teachers are constructing work for their students who engage in habits of mind and thinking deeper about instruction, it crosses those invisible lines. GCISD instructional specialists/coaches are master teachers in their content area and pedagogy. Their belief is that if you are a reflective learner, you can learn about robotics and engineering as needed.

Kimberly Lane is a blended technology coach working at the district level in Lancaster ISD. In the district-wide STEM program, technology coaches are considered part of the instructional team but are deployed from central administration. As a coach working with technology, Lane considers herself as part of the STEM team. What she does from her standpoint is to find out from teachers, "What do you need help with?"

Being with administration is not a hindrance, but to be effective Lane needs to be on campus, very observant, and focused on finding out what she can do to enhance the students' and teachers' learning experience. Lane is able to bring the authentic technology piece into a PBL. She shares with teachers how she is able to research technology utilization information on the technical side. She has skills in Photoshop, ProLogic, coding, and for aligning the technology use to their content areas, to enhance science and math instruction. She works only with teachers but finds her assistance makes working with students on technology much easier for the teacher.

According to Lane, "The benefit of not being part of campus administration is that teachers want to speak with me if they have a problem; if I see something I can do in their classroom, they don't have to go through campus administration to get it done." Lane works to gain teachers' trust by working with them as much as she can. She checks in with the campus coaches and content specialists to see if there are things they need her to do to help teachers gain skills in technology usage. Lane sees herself as the middleman and ultimately her role is to assist teachers as they assist their students. "I will work late nights to help them; that understanding is a huge plus if they are to see me as a coach."

Marisa Guzman is a math–science instructional coach for a K-5 campus in Katy ISD. Although she is not on a STEM campus, her role is in helping the teachers to integrate quality STEM instructional practices into their pedagogy and lesson. According to Guzman, "It is becoming more and more popular to talk about STEM because of the technology part of it. On my campus STEM is not just about science and math, with technology and engineering added in, but it is how the four disciplines come together in the real world."

In Katy ISD, instructional coaches are part of the administration team, but each is assigned to a campus. Teachers recognize Guzman as part of their instructional team. That is an advantage because the perception is that she is "on their side." Her job is to help them and they trust her to do that. Marisa coaches science and math, but she says, "Honestly, because of the new math standards I feel more like a math coach; to provide the most support I could I had to be creative." So, on Monday and Tuesday her focus is on science; modeling strategies and co-teaching when when they focus on something new. But, because of the stress caused by implementing new math standards, the focus is shifting towards coaching strategies for math rather than science. Wednesdays through Fridays she is in the science lab monitoring STEM implementation and observing student engagement.

As the math–science coach, Guzman would admit she is still working through some roadblocks as a STEM coach; such as the lack of time. It is the lack of STEM time. With so much coming "top down" in the way of content from district initiatives, there is not enough time in the week to discuss STEM integration and curriculum with each grade level. There are two coaches on her campus. So as the campus instructional coaching team they decided to push literacy into science and math. She convinced the third through fifth grade reading teachers to pull out the mini-science nonfiction text and make it a station, so that even during a math workshop students can be reading science as well. The science and math teachers communicate with the reading teachers by checking in on the questions they are asking their students about the math and science contents of the books.

As the STEM-based math–science instructional coach Guzman finds that engineering is the perfect way to learn how the NGSS and *A Framework for K-12 Science Education* (NRC, 2012) look at integrating engineering. Guzman works with teachers to solve problems and participate in challenging tasks. They plan lessons together for their students to use an engineering design process (EDP), collect data, ask questions, and share results with everyone.

The Harmony Public Schools of Dallas, a public charter school located in the DFW Metroplex, began using STEM coaches several years ago. Dillon Chevalier was selected to join the first cadre of coaches who were deployed from the district level but worked in each STEM academy with teachers as a coach. He was considered part of the administration because he was centrally deployed, but he did not do teacher evaluations, which most administrators did. He considered that an important aspect of his role as coach.

> Because when you add that layer it can become a different relationship. I think principals and coaches should work together, but teachers may become uncomfortable if all of their observation data and feedback is being discussed with principals. My coaching role was separate from evaluations, which allowed the teachers and I to remain on the same team.

When he became a STEM coach, he and the coaching cadre began investigating different coaching models and the superintendent was fully supportive as the cadre members were providing recommendations for how the coaching program would emerge. They were learning as they went along as well. They were creating the goals and the program outcomes as they were building the program. According to Chevalier, "I think the way our superintendent began utilizing us as a team to develop a program was great." He knew they would be effective because of their expertise as classroom teachers and their prior campus leadership in their content areas.

The cadre recognized that they had an opportunity to impact teacher instructional quality and to promote implementation of STEM-based practices such as PBLs. Chevalier was able to attend training sessions for coaches and knew if he had requested, the district would have sent him to more; but as he was gaining an understanding of the role of coaching he became aware of the many resources available.

As a coach he was busy from the start, scheduling observations and following up with conversations. There wasn't any set expectation for teachers to utilize coaching but the coaches did need to meet with each teacher a certain number of times. Chevalier would schedule visits and observations and wait for confirmation. He worked with teachers to schedule them. Sometimes when he arrived, he could tell it was a bad time or bad day for them, so he would stop the observation and reschedule for a better time. In Chevalier's opinion, there are many things on a teacher's plate and perhaps your being there put them in an uncomfortable position because they were not at their best:

> I made myself accessible—If I had an observation or coaching session scheduled, but noticed it ended up being a bad time for the teacher I would simply reschedule. I found it beneficial to make sure the teacher was comfortable and ready for observations and conversations. I used to think coaching had to be one-on-one sessions with a lot of structure to be effective. However, I found that many of my productive interactions with teachers were at the spur of the moment such as between class periods, during a break, or in the teachers' lounge. They would grab my sleeve and ask "How about this?"

Part of Chevalier's responsibilities in his role as coach was to provide professional development to the science teachers he was coaching. He saw coaching and PD as extensions of each other, but he liked the PD portion the best. During in-service PD sessions at the start of the school year, the teachers could see his personality and found he had an ability to build rapport with most of them. They were able to determine that his choice of topics were important and that he did not have them doing things to fill or waste their time. He shared with them things about STEM that could be of value and useful to them. This initial PD gave him the opportunity to start their relationships off on the right foot and to be seen as someone who could be called on to support them in their role as a STEM instructor.

In Chevalier's opinion, PD impacted student achievement without him needing to actually be in every teacher's classroom. He found he enjoyed working with adults and helping them to improve their practices for the benefits of the students in their classrooms.

STEM Coaches as Teachers

While teaching at a STEM middle school academy in Folsom, California, Debra Krikourian is the district's STEM lead teacher and a Project Lead the Way (PLTW) trainer and coach. Her STEM academy is a school-within-a-school model, where the academy is located on a larger middle school campus that is not STEM-focused. PLTW is one of the ways Krikourian's campus brings problem-solving and engineering design into their academy. She became a coach for PLTW because of her love for all disciplines of STEM and her desire to help students and teachers understand why STEM is important in their culture.

In Krikourian's opinion there is a need to redirect the education pipeline so that more students become interested in STEM careers and keep that interest through high school:

> Currently in education teachers are focusing the pipeline into different areas. Students coming up from elementary are excited about STEM, but somehow in middle school it gets the STEM pipeline plugged up. At HS we need to get kids involved and keep them in the pipeline by getting them involved in STEM courses and careers.

In order to prepare students for college and to maintain their skills in learning at a more rigorous level, changes are required at the middle school and high school levels. Students and parents need to recognize that problem-solving skills and critical thinking rather than transcripts and grade point average (GPA) should be the focus for learning.

To make that happen involves coaches sharing with teachers the tools for a design process, helping them create projects with goals that will allow students to fail and to redesign. These types of projects may take longer than they anticipate but they can gain validity along the way. By coaching teachers in ways to allow students to self-assess, they will learn to be judges of the quality of their own work. One of the ways this can be accomplished is by PBL through real-life scenarios using science, technology, engineering, and math to answer and solve problems.

The California Department of Education adopted the NGSS as the basis of their science standards. Krikourian sees that as a good starting point for a STEM focus. In California, all science teachers are beginning to know what is involved in STEM; engineering, computer, and math are part of it. Engineering design and building though geometry connects the math. Krikourian thinks teachers who are new to STEM need support and coaching to help them think about their content differently, to take action, and to give them the tools they need to begin implementation. Krikourian believes, "Our kids are learning differently and they are different than even a generation ago."

Krikourian suggests that elementary teachers focus on solving problems rather than a literacy based focus:

> She says it may be more exciting to look at Jack and the Beanstalk for structure and function; what was his goal and what problems would he encounter and solve along the way? Then building something from everyday materials that would be able to hold Jack up. Measuring their model with units and writing about what they did and why. These are a big part of bringing STEM into your classroom.

As a STEM coach and PTLW instructor Krikourian works with teachers in her STEM academy and goes out to other schools as a PTLW consultant to model instructional strategies and coach the lessons teachers will use in real-life problem-solving and data-gathering in the curriculum disciplines.

STEM Coaching Consultants

As the STEM-based campus principal evaluates the capacity of her faculty, their expertise in STEM practices, knowledge of technology applications, and the limited nature of district resources in STEM practices, it may become apparent that there is a need to seek resources and assistance from outside the district. This is often the case when bringing forward initiatives that may have already tapped out the expertise that is found within the district's organization. On other occasions they find it may be expedient either to bring in professional consultants or to send teachers outside the district to PD sessions, conferences, or training to move their initiatives forward.

Some areas where STEM consultants or outside STEM professional development venues are most effective include:

◆ Technology integration
◆ Initiation to practices that are unique to STEM, such as:
  ● Project-based learning
  ● Engineering design experiences
  ● Differentiation for unique student groups, such as
    ○ Accelerated or advanced learners
    ○ Gifted and talented students
    ○ Non-motivated learners
    ○ Students with learning disabilities.

Janelle McLaughlin is a STEM consultant with a software company who specifically works with forward-thinking STEM campuses to help them integrate software packages into STEM-related instructional practices. As she sees it, STEM is looking at the fields of science and mathematics and creating interrelatedness through technology and engineering:

> STEM is a combination of workforce initiatives and good instructional practice. STEM resources should specifically look for concepts that can blend. The important part is not where it was initiated or why it is now in the spotlight; it is about making it happen in classrooms today!

Coming from an elementary background, McLaughlin knows that all knowledge is interrelated. It is in the upper grades that concepts get broken down into silos. Being in the education technology industry, she believes it can be a vehicle for change in that area.

McLaughlin is now professionally coaching and consulting, and working with school districts all over the US. In this role she creates partnerships with schools through a professional learning plan. She works with cohorts within each organization to integrate best instructional practices into their operations. A typical cohort has around 20 teachers. The first step is about setting up the infrastructure for success and working with teachers through whole-group workshops to create an awareness of what they can accomplish. She then begins meeting one-on-one with teachers, within each cohort, to coach and model the use of the strategies. In her coaching cycle they move from whole group to one-on-one sessions very quickly.

McLaughlin has found there is a greater probability for teachers to continue with an instructional practice when coaching is provided. Coaching is needed for the added support required by each teacher to differentiate the practice to meet their own learning style, teaching disposition, and the need of the students they teach.

Science Instructional Specialist

As an outstanding teacher, you have been selected to serve as a science teacher specialist because you stood out among the ranks of the science teachers on your campus and in your district. Because of your reputation as a knowledgeable science instructor and the scores your students get on their common assessments, you have been asked to share your secrets to student success with your peers to help them do the same with their students' scores.

As a content specialist you are expected to have extensive knowledge of the state standards and the assessments used to judge mastery of the content across grade-level bands. A clear understanding of the vertical alignment of the content is used as standards are broken down into units of instruction for the curriculum used by teachers at each grade level. Your rich background in science teaching has also helped you to test, utilize, analyze, and implement the most effective instructional strategies for diverse groups of students. This "toolkit" is one that you will share with your campus science teachers on a regular basis, through PLC groups, professional development sessions and workshops, one-on-one sessions with teachers, and perhaps at conferences.

In some districts, constructing content-based assessments that are administered at the end of units or at the semester is one of your responsibilities. These assessments are intended to provide a benchmark of student mastery of the concepts, but also to reveal where students will need to revisit content prior to the state assessments or the end of course exams. The value of this comes as you are assisting teachers in planning how to include additional strategies and resources to assist their students in mastering the more difficult concepts that are revealed through data analysis of unit tests and semester exams.

As some coaches have already found, there is a need for instructional strategies, resources, and materials that help teachers when reviewing for the state assessments. Coaches work to pair high-quality instructional strategies with the resources and materials chosen or written. In some districts, the science instructional specialists create these, and, in others, ready-made materials are purchased from online publishers.

Whether you serve as a coach or mentor depends on the experience of the teachers you are working with. When working with teachers who are new to teaching science, you will be acting as a mentor, working to bridge their craft knowledge and content knowledge until they have a firm grasp on their content and the best and most effective strategies to use while teaching it. You may serve as a mentor for most of their initial school year and for some into their second year, slowly removing the scaffolding of support so they will eventually need your help and advice less often. Instructional mentors may need to teach them the content and also how to break it down to an age-appropriate level for their students, help them plan their lessons, provide suggestions for which strategies work best for teaching that concept, perhaps model or co-teach with them, and then to reflect with them on how the lesson went after it is taught.

When working with experienced teachers who are just new to the grade level, you most likely will serve as a coach, sharing the location of resources, and working with them in their grade-level team to share research-based strategies and assessment data to help them in planning instructional units and lessons. Caution should be taken when working with experienced teachers in assuming they do not have a grasp of the most effective instructional strategies or content knowledge. Using a coaching stance rather than that of a mentor provides an opportunity to ask questions about their plans and intentions and to listen carefully for their thoughtful responses about their selections. Through coaching conversations you show them your respect for their expertise and then think with them as they formulate their plans for incorporating the most effective strategies and practices for the success of their students.

Sharry Whitney was an instructional coach before moving to the district level. Her pathway from the seventh grade science classroom to the district was filled with many insights. The district recognized that coaches needed training in how to help teachers, so they were providing a variety of training. During that first year Whitney went to training at *Just For Kids* and at the Charles A. Dana Center in Austin, TX. According to Whitney, "I read more than I have ever read in my life about how to be a successful coach and the education research about science instructional strategies and Best Practices." Some of her resources were publications from *Ed Leadership*, the educational journal from ASCD, and books recommended through the training courses she attended.

Whitney credits her success as an instructional coach to her opportunity to be mentored and coached by veteran coaches. They provided a level of PD that training sessions did not. Master coaches provided their perspective of coaching in real life and shared how they learned to handle difficult situations with teachers and administrators. She called these important lessons, "The Tips and Tricks of the Trade."

> I also had a lot of OJT, On the Job Training! Talking with teachers made me realize that we were learning together. I was building relationships with them because I was in it with them. Learning about the diversity of each of the campuses I served, was not covered in my training. The differing cultures and norms of each campus was unexpected by me but a valuable lesson.

As a teacher, Whitney didn't realize what a difference a principal makes to a campus compared to the difference a single teacher can make. According to Whitney, "walking classrooms was an eye opener; as a teacher I never saw other teachers teach." In her first year of coaching she considers walking classrooms and seeing other teachers' teaching was most valuable. She discovered there is a need to allow and make time for teachers to observe their fellow teachers: it is so powerful. It is evident what is working and what is not working for students.

As a coach, she collaborated with teachers as they planned their lessons, helping them to embed best practices. Whitney would co-teach some lessons with them. She would "walk classrooms" during the school day to see what teachers needed through observing their practice. In follow-up conversations, she would offer to model the instructional strategies that would perhaps be more effective or would offer co-teach during their classes if desired by the teacher:

> In the end though, the majority of my time became data crunching. I would analyze the student results of the curriculum-based assessments. After looking at student results, and trends in the numbers, I needed to decide how to enter into a discussion with each teacher about their data. That transition happened over the course of my first year as a science instructional coach.

Student data meetings were scheduled with teachers. It was cumbersome and difficult. There was a lot of resistance in getting teachers to schedule these with her. In looking for a way to break through, "I realized I needed to say, I am here to help you." Even though they heard what she said worked or did not work, they would not take her advice. She found that many experienced and novice teachers discounted her experiences and expertise. Every teacher is quite certain that his or her students and teaching situations are unique. Whitney learned she should not provide advice and needed to help each teacher think more deeply about their own practice, allowing them to come to their own solution:

> Interestingly, now looking back over my 28 years of being a teacher, coach, and administrator, that no matter the economics, race, or needs of a set of students, students are students and they all have similar needs. The key in meeting your students' needs is allowing for their uniqueness within the classroom. What you have to provide, as the teacher, is differentiation. You first know your students then provide each student and/ or groups of students the learning opportunities that meet their needs. Teachers need to be well versed in differentiated instructional strategies and their ability to prepare learning opportunities for their students' choice and voice.

Technology Instructional Specialist

In order for a STEM program to have all the pieces in place for an integrated STEM learning environment many districts provide a technology instructional specialist to work with teachers for the seamless integration of technology. Some districts provide support to campuses through a district-deployed STEM coach for technology, specifically for the integration of technology into science and math courses. In the Grapevine-Colleyville ISD, Joe Todd provides that support in his role as a secondary instructional coach. With Todd's extensive experience in inquiry and hands-on science and his background in instructional lab technology, he brings a wealth of practical application to the STEM classroom. According to Todd:

> STEM is an educational approach to connect students to the real world of the future. It is to use technology to design solutions, to engineer solutions, and to see the connections in the real world. The integration of math, reading, and writing all fall into place when they are used to understand the nature of the solution they are developing.

Todd works with the district's science director, to outline the technology integration goals on which he is to focus. They meet regularly to review the district goals in order of tiers to determine priority. Overall, his goals focus on the integration of inquiry into science lessons and for more student ownership of what they are to learn. As a large part of his science STEM focus, Todd works to integrate the best instructional practices for science and student use of academic vocabulary. He boils it down to:

> For me, the integration of technology is a priority. The use of technology has changed dramatically in the world. Hospitals, for instance, no longer use glass thermometers. Instead, they use digital thermometers and pulse oximeters. Modernization of science instruction includes best practices for media use and acquisition, and doing hands on experiments that integrate technology.

> I work to incorporate technology into science investigations and help teachers within digital cadres. The teachers may have Chromebooks or are learning to use tools in a digital environment to quantify phenomenon and to foster communication and collaboration. I am part of an initiative with many baby steps. I do trainings in the use of sensors for integration into science and math.

Math, ELA, and Other Content Area Instructional Coaches

Many larger districts such as GCISD used to have content area teaching specialists, but now, as district-deployed positions, the specialist roles have expanded and they are providing higher levels of instructional support. As a result they are called instructional coaches. To reverse the trend in teacher turnover, the district has provided instructional coaches to meet with all new teachers weekly. Some teachers who are new to the district are experienced and have taught two to four years; they are also provided a coach. So, for those who are new to the district, there is an understanding when they are hired they will work with coaches. Todd works with all teachers and gets to work with experienced teachers who are new to technology.

> I work with teachers who have at-risk and English language learners in their classes. I bring up about their differentiated practices and the data to help them think about using practices that benefit all kids and especially for those who are struggling.

As district deployed instructional coaches, their roles are broader but their narrowly focused goals are to support district initiatives for the implementation of STEM instructional practices in such a way that teachers have an impact on student success and academic achievement. Dr. Leslie Hancock is an ELA instructional coach who is part of the GCISD C&I team but is assigned specifically to one of the district's high school campuses.

Hancock, as a high school instructional coach, was given a nebulous list of responsibilities as she began her role as campus liaison and instructional coach, so she became creative. As a coach she developed several metrics to track teacher growth for such phenomena as students' active involvement, engagement, task complexity, as well as types of teacher feedback. Through observations and feedback, Hancock was able to increase teacher implementation of strategies, which resulted in increases in active involvement and engagement, higher levels of task complexity, and more constructive teacher feedback.

One of Grapevine High School's foci is the AVID (Advancement Via Individual Determination) program, which was adopted by the district as a means of supporting students in STEM and the other disciplines. At Hancock's campus the leadership team chose to offer the AVID elective course while promoting AVID school-wide. All teachers employ WICOR strategies throughout every content area. WICOR strategies fall under the following umbrellas: Writing, Inquiry, Collaboration, Organization, and

Reading. The AVID elective instructors meet with students every other day and focus on equipping them with the habits and skills that will prepare them for college. All teachers are systematically trained in the WICOR strategies and those tenets organize the teacher training. The AVID electives and school-wide initiative are already showing results in terms of accountability ratings in attendance, academic achievement, and college acceptance.

Initially, Hancock had always been a supporter of good teaching practices, but needed to vet the best practices research on her own. She had been aware of it for many years, and did additional research into the AVID program and made the decision for herself. Many teachers just like her stated that the school was already using inquiry and collaboration for years. They were doing the activities already. But, through doing comparisons, she found the strategies used were neither as specific nor as structured. To change student engagement and involvement there needed to be the same definitions, understandings, and utilization by all. She agreed that they were not new but now they needed to be refined.

In Hancock's district all new hires are required to work with an instructional coach during their first year or two with the district. This induction time is provided for new teachers to learn about the culture and initiatives of the district and to be supported in learning how to meet the standards for implementing quality instructional practices that are to occur in every classroom every day. Veteran teachers are also supported but not in such a structured format. Coaching is not just for novices to the field of education but also for those who want to change or adjust their instructional practice. Because there are over 100 teachers and only one of her, most of Hancock's time is spent with the 30 teachers that are new to the campus this year.

Some of the coaching for veteran teachers includes integration of Google education tools (Google Drive and Google Classroom). They learn together how to use Google Drive to enhance instruction. Hancock's campus has instructional technology coaches to support the campus goal for integration of technology into instruction and they are the go-to team for teaching about advanced topics in instructional technology.

The STEM coach's role is specifically designed to support teachers in meeting all expectations to integrate science, math, engineering, and technology with 21st Century Skills in authentic, aligned, and autonomous ways. The STEM coach is an important component of the K-12 system, with a clear understanding of the need for STEM qualified graduates. Coaching has become one of the key factors in teachers' ability to improve their instructional practice.

Part I

Summary, Conclusion, and Resources

In Part I care has been taken to build an understanding of how STEM and a STEM-based instructional program is different than that of a traditional instructional approach taken by a teacher or campus when looking at the strategies and lens for content delivery. The outcomes for students take on a new meaning when the curriculum and content are viewed through a STEM lens.

When a campus or district adopts a STEM model, many changes need to occur. As educational research has shown, change is hard. Systems of supports need to be in place not only for changing teacher instructional practice, but also for addressing student academic needs which were probably the impetus for the change. The STEM coach at all levels, from state agencies to campus-based instructional specialists, has a role in making the transition systematic, effective, and beneficial.

Part II focuses on the strategies STEM coaches use when fulfilling their role as the campus expert on STEM-based instruction. Highlights include: building a relationship based on trust with teachers, working with teachers in their classrooms, planning STEM-focused lessons, professional learning, and the coaching cycle.

Resources

References

Achieve, Inc. (2013). *Next Generation Science Standards* (NGSS). Washington, DC: National Academies Press.

Association for Supervision and Curriculum Development (ASCD). *Educational Leadership* (*Ed Leadership*), monthly magazine.

Erickson, Lynn (2008). *Stirring the Head, Heart, and Soul: Redefining Curriculum, Instruction, and Concept-Based Learning*. Thousand Oaks, CA: Corwin Press.

Frontier, Tony and Rickabaugh, James (2014). *Five Levers to Improve Learning: How to Prioritize for Powerful School Results*. Alexandria, VA: ASCD.

Heath, Chip and Heath, Dan (2010). *Switch: How to Change Things When Change Is Hard*. New York: Broadway Books.

Hord, Shirley M., Rutherford, William L., Huling-Austin, Leslie, Hall, Gene E., and Knoll, Marcia Kalb (1987; revd 2006). *Taking Charge of Change*. Alexandria, VA: ASCD.

Knight, Jim (2011). *Unmistakable Impact: A Partnership Approach for Dramatically Improving Instruction*. Thousand Oaks, CA: Corwin Press and LearningForward.

National Research Council (NRC) (2012). *A Framework for K-12 Science Education*. Washington, DC: National Academies Press.

Schmoker, Mike (2015). Time to Restructure Teacher Professional Development. *Education Week* (October 20), www.edweek.org/ew/articles/2015/10/21/its-time-to-restructure-teacher-professional-development.html

Websites

◆ *21st Century Skills*, www.p21.org/
◆ *A Framework for K-12 Science Education*, www.nextgenscience.org/framework-k%E2%80%9312-science-education
◆ *ACT: Solutions for K-12 Education, College, And Career Readiness*, www.act.org/research/policymakers/pdf/Work-Readiness-Standards-and-Benchmarks.pdf
◆ *Cognitive Coaching (CC) by Arthur Costa and Robert Garmston*, www.thinkingcollaborative.com/
◆ *Common Core*, www.corestandards.org/ELA-Literacy/CCRA/R/
◆ *Engineering Is Elementary (EIE) from the Science Museum of Boston*, www.eie.org/
◆ *Leading Forward—Action Driven 2021 (LEAD 2021) Grapevine-Colleyville Independent School District Strategic Plan*, www.gcisd-k12.org/lead2021
◆ *Next Generation Science Standards* (NGSS), www.nextgenscience.org/
◆ *Revisiting the STEM Workforce*, www.nssf.gov/nsb/publications/2015/nab201510.pdf
◆ *Texas Science, Technology, Engineering and Mathematics (T-STEM) Design Blueprint*, www.tstemblueprint.org
◆ *The Mirage: Confronting the Hard Truth About Our Quest for Teacher Development*, http://tntp.org/publications/view/the-mirage-confronting-the-truth-about-our-quest-for-teacher-development

Organization websites

◆ Change The Equation—www.changetheequation.org
◆ National Science Board (NSB)—www.nsf.gov/nsb/

- ◆ ACT—www.ACT.org (The organization has changed its name to ACT and the initials no longer have meaning.)
- ◆ Partnership For 21st Century Skills (P21)—www.p21.org/
- ◆ The New Teacher Project (TNTP)—www.tntp.org
- ◆ Code.org®—www.code.org
- ◆ ASCD (Professional Learning And Community For Educators)—www.ascd.org
- ◆ Institute For Learning—http://ifl.pitt.edu/
- ◆ STEMx Network—www.STEMx.org
- ◆ Educate Texas—www.edtx.org
- ◆ K20 Center For Educational And Community Renewal At The University Of Oklahoma—www.k20center.ou.edu
- ◆ Just For Kids—www.edresults.org
- ◆ Charles A. Dana Center—www.utdanacenter.org
- ◆ Association For Supervision And Curriculum Development (ASCD)—www.ascd.org

Part II

The Practices of a STEM Coach

Part II shares what I have learned as a STEM coach as well as the insights of fellow STEM coaches and colleagues as they have grown in the mastery of their skills. Using coaching and mentoring strategies moves traditional teachers and administrators through the micro-movements needed for real, measurable, and sustainable changes towards more effective STEM practices. It changes the way educators think about student growth and development. The metacognition required in coaching deepens the experience and makes it more than a review of lesson plans, going over data, or the sharing of resources. It is about mindsets, habits of thinking, and achieving goals through intentional actions that develop as an outgrowth of a coaching conversation.

Part II shares those strategies as well as offering suggestions, such as when it becomes important to switch to mentoring conversations from coaching. Based on the expertise of the person you are coaching, shifting between the two types of conversation should be transparent and intentional. For the care and maintenance of the fragile relationship you are building, it is most important to know the expertise in content knowledge and instruction practices of the teacher or administrator you are working with, before you select your strategy.

Part II focuses not on the instructional strategies about specific content areas, such as science, math, or ELA, but on those strategies for you as a STEM coach to bring STEM into the classroom as an authentic tool for student achievement.

7

Building the Relationship First

Leslie Hancock has a doctorate in curriculum and instruction. A portion of her studies at the doctorate level were the instructional strategies that go across curricular boundaries such as cooperative learning, quality questioning, wait time, and the value of a positive learning culture in a classroom. As a generalist teacher, she has had first-hand experiences in the use of these strategies and how well they can be adapted within the different student groups and achievement levels she taught in her own classrooms.

One of the learning theories Hancock has adopted is about mindset and the willingness people have to consider new ideas and challenges. Mindset can be one of the reasons teachers hesitate in trying new instructional strategies. In her studies she has spent time in learning how people learn. She has no hesitation supporting STEM instruction and fully supports teachers' growth in that area when asked for her help in doing so.

When Hancock enters a science or math classroom she knows she is in an arena of an expert, so by demonstrating extreme deference to the teacher's understanding of their own content she does not step on toes. As Hancock relates, "For example, I am very careful of how I enter into a physics classroom. My orientation: 'This is all about you, your students, your content, and your practice.' If our coaching conversation delves too deeply into content-specific territory, I refer the teacher to a content area coach."

Build Trust by Starting Where They Are

In her role, as director of STEM and Curriculum Innovation in Lancaster ISD, Kyndra Johnson believes in servant-leadership. She and her team have become valued as resources by the principals and teachers because of this attitude. They built strong relationships because of their reliability and credibility in their desire to serve. It is her philosophy to accept and acknowledge people where they are and support them in their growth. Johnson states:

> If a person feels diminished through your words or actions, you will make them believe they have deficits. You will be unable to influence their thoughts or actions. By meeting them where they are, and through a servant leader role, you have the most influence in changing their thinking and practice.
>
> It is not about what you know and the tools you use. It is about finding their strengths, recognizing the tools they use, and helping them grow to be more effective. It is by understanding that in a relationship between coach and teacher, you are the resources and you serve as a thinking partner.

Johnson feels her role, as a coach to coaches, is not to impart knowledge and wisdom, but to help exercise more fully the strengths a coach, teacher, or principal already has. It is to help them discover how they can use their strengths to accomplish what they need to do and what is expected. Coaching is not about giving away what you know, but knowing how to support the person you are coaching for their growth.

When to Coach and When to Mentor

When the Lancaster ISD coaches are working with teachers who are struggling to bring student achievement forward, Kyndra Johnson advises them to provide more intentional support. Sometimes the teachers they are coaching have not tried more effective strategies with their struggling students or don't know how to help their students. Using the coaching model alone may not work, because they don't have enough experience within themselves to generate ideas. Perhaps, they haven't had a feeling of accomplishment with students for a long time. They can grow in developmentally small steps. In order to encourage the teachers' professional growth Johnson suggests helping them to recognize small increments of growth. Being innovative and creative in your approach and having faith in their abilities will build the relationship so that you can impact their thinking and their productivity.

Marisa Guzman, the math and science coach in Katy ISD, has grown professionally in her role. During her first year she found herself mainly assisting teachers and working with students. She would plan with teachers each week, but because of testing and creating tests for small groups she was in the classroom less than she thought she should be. An additional limitation Guzman ran into was that sometimes teachers would not let her into their rooms because they didn't know why she needed to be there. "I needed to be resourceful, so that they would invite me in. I created interactive boards for them and would hang out in their rooms on several occasions working with students and helping out at stations to co-teach lessons, and modeling the lessons they are not comfortable with. Now they are extremely welcoming. They trust me and we have a great relationship."

New Teacher Mentor

Research supporting mentoring programs for induction-year teachers can be found in a 2011 report by Ingersoll and Strong in the *Review of Education Research*. This study examines 15 published studies on the effects of teacher induction and mentoring programs, and points out:

> For classroom instructional practices, the majority of studies reviewed showed that beginning teachers who participated in some kind of induction performed better at various aspects of teaching, such as keeping students on task, developing workable lesson plans, using effective student questioning practices, adjusting classroom activities to meet students' interests, maintaining a positive classroom atmosphere, and demonstrating successful classroom management.

The mentors' roles include sharing insight gained from experience, stimulating new ideas, demonstrating effective classroom management, and organizing classroom and lab supplies. Novice teachers in their induction year are learning their craft. Induction-year teachers typically fall into two categories: university certified or alternatively certified. A mentor relationship can benefit both groups.

Teachers in the first group are usually recent college graduates who have been in pre-service university programs and have had an opportunity to participate in a practicum for a period of time. Student teaching, as it was once called, can be from six weeks to a semester in a classroom with a cooperating teacher and coached by a supervising teacher from their university program. These novice teachers will enter the classroom for the first time with a degree in the field they are teaching and with teaching credentials.

The second group of induction-year teachers is typically more mature in age and life experiences. These teachers include college graduates with an expertise in content knowledge and practical applications of it. They are seeking alternative certification in teaching, through an abbreviated program. Alternative certification, or as it is sometimes called emergency certification, requires generalized courses in pedagogy and lesson design. In a standard program these courses are taken on weekends and for a brief program in the summer either before or after the initial teaching experience. Often such teachers do not receive their teaching credentials until after completion of their induction year.

Teachers holding an alternative teaching certificate are as dedicated and caring as those who go through a pre-service program, but often lack the first-hand experience that working with a cooperating teacher and her students can provide. They are limited in perspective of how to use the strategies and methods that were provided in their coursework. Often they are unable to relate to current classroom practice because their only perspective is based on instructional experiences from when they were K-12 students and in college. Although rich in science or math content knowledge and perhaps having experience in a STEM field through employment, they do not have a variety of instructional and management strategies to use as they try to share their knowledge and expertise with students.

The role of a mentor is to fill in the gaps of either content knowledge or pedagogy that may not be integrated into novice teachers' craft knowledge yet. Mentors provide scaffolding that will eventually no longer be needed. Scaffolding usually includes resources and suggestions about instructional strategies to try with their students and to add to the portfolios of practice. Coaching is not effective with novice teachers because they have not had enough experience to gather the expertise required for all the situations that could possibly be in store for them—situations apart from teaching, such as setting up their grading criteria, planning for differentiated lessons for ELL students, budgeting their limited resources for classroom materials, setting up their classrooms for efficiency, access to all students, classroom management techniques, preparing for a substitute teacher, and the list goes on.

Also the role of mentor is to acclimate novice teachers to the culture of the education profession that does not limit its demands to the hours that school is in session. Those unlimited responsibilities and time demands come from planning thoughtful instruction, evaluating student work, and assessing student mastery of content. Meeting these responsibilities requires knowing and responding to the differentiated abilities and levels of the students who are now in their charge. It also requires additional hours after the official school day.

New teachers will be overwhelmed at the start. A knowledgeable mentor provides a predictable forecast of the ebb and flow of the school year, which helps them to anticipate when those times will fall and to plan for them. Busy times are those such as at the end of a grading period, before a school holiday, parent–teacher conferences, and of course when flu season hits.

Other supports provided by a mentor include a variety of roles, depending on the stresses on the new teacher at the time. These can include being a sounding board when they are frustrated, a confidante when they voicing their frustrations about working with team members, a cheerleader when they need encouragement or are overwhelmed, an advisor when discussing the pros and cons of sharing social media with students, and a teacher when they just don't know what they need to know to do the best for their students.

When it comes to STEM instructional practices, your role becomes even more important, because these may be new ideas to them and not what they have already experienced. As their mentor you will need to guide them in the development of their instructional philosophy, their beliefs about instruction and teaching. For STEM to become part of their philosophy they need to understand the "why" for all instruction to be viewed through an interdisciplinary STEM lens, and the "how" to thoughtfully layer STEM strategies and 21st Century Skills into their lesson designs and instruction.

"STEM-ification" of an instruction philosophy includes teaching with a hands-on approach through inquiry. The new teachers will need help in moving from a behaviorist approach to a constructivist approach in thinking, teaching, and learning. This includes finding ways for developing curiosity in students to use critical thinking as they innovate the solutions to authentic, real-world problems through engineering. Utilizing project-based learning as a key to STEM instruction can serve as the vehicle for students to use an interdisciplinary approach to the problem. It gives them autonomy in voice and choice as they develop their solutions.

The true enjoyment of being a mentor is when the lens of STEM begins with your teaching and checking for use in the novice teachers' instructional plans, but becomes the framework for their thinking and being a STEM teacher. When asking Jodi Marchesso, of Pasadena USC, what she does on a regular basis, she comments jokingly that she is still trying to figure that out. Every person she coaches is different. Everyone needs to be approached in a different way. They all have different beliefs and experiences where they are coming from:

This year I am focusing on the new teachers. Those fresh out of college often need extra support with content and I mentor them. Many of the experienced teachers who are new to the district are experts in content so I approach them differently, mostly through coaching. It is important to remember that coaching and mentoring are based on changing beliefs in order to change instruction. Everyone's beliefs are different.

Marchesso usually begins by meeting with teachers during their prep period or after school to have a sit-down, face-to-face discussion. She doesn't begin with observations because in her opinion that requires a huge trust bridge. Trust needs to be there before she can walk into their classroom to give feedback that they will appreciate.

Most new teachers want to meet weekly to plan. Her schedule does not allow enough time for that and to serve them all. She does however meet with each new teacher bi-monthly and every conversation is 30–60 minutes. Often when the teacher determines the topic of the meeting it is on classroom management, but the focus should be on STEM instructional strategies:

I know that good, engaging instruction will drive behavior management; it comes with it. So, if I find we can't get into instruction because of management concerns, I change the focus of our conversations to instruction. Good instruction decreases management issues.

The next step is to watch the teachers in action. So if, after a few meetings, they have not invited Marchesso to visit their classroom or if they decline her offer to visit because they continue to have the same issues, then she will request to come in to watch the class in action.

How much time I spend depends on the situation. I'm the only science coach for the district and I'm K-12. The district has deployed a total of 9 coaches; there is me for STEM/science, two math coaches at the secondary level, three elementary ELA and math coaches, and two secondary literacy coaches. In our district office the philosophy is teacher initiated coaching. It is available for any teacher that wants help.

Marchesso's primary activity has been as a curriculum specialist in years past. Fortunately for her, most science teachers in the Pasadena USD are veterans with five or more years of teaching experience. But, this is the first year with a large number of new teachers due to a large number of retirees. Now she finds that she spends most of her time mentoring with new teachers. In her opinion, the NGSS transition needs to be coming through her lens for

STEM at the start of their first year in Pasadena USD. It is important for them to get their instructional strategies right, so she is working very closely with them. She believes it is imperative for their inductees to not teach from misunderstandings about STEM but to learn how to teach hands-on, inquiry-based STEM-based science.

Address Their Concerns Before Addressing Their Instruction

Sharry Whitney shared a story about one of the science teachers she was coaching who was in the seventh grade professional learning community (PLC) she set up at the district level:

> I judge my success as a coach by the changes I see in teachers, one teacher at a time. One specific time I can share was for a new middle school teacher. Teaching was her second career. She was assigned as the second seventh grade science teacher for her campus. For some reason, the other seventh grade teacher on her campus absolutely refused to meet, share resources, or plan lessons with her. The novice teacher reached out to me because she was scared, unsure, and didn't know what to do. Because I had been a seventh grade science teacher I brought her my book of resources. It had lots of templates and things that I had developed that met the standards and were successful with my students.
>
> I then put her in contact with a group of seventh grade teachers at a nearby middle school. They supported her. She talked with them on the phone, through emails, and met with them several times throughout the year. I continued to meet with her as well and we developed a supporting relationship. She sent her principal and me a letter saying how much she appreciated my support as her coach. She discussed the value of our relationship and the things I provided.

According to Whitney, "Behind the scenes I met with her principal to discuss the lack of collegiality by her seventh grade teaching peer." There may have been many reasons for the lack of willingness to be collegial. In an effort to correct the situation, the following year, the non-collegial teacher was assigned to another grade level. A new teacher was moved into seventh grade and a collaborative relationship was formed. The campus could have lost a good teacher out of her sheer frustration. The three pieces—a coach, support group, and responsive administration—came together and helped the novice to become an effective and successful teacher. Rather than providing advice first, her coach spent the time to address her concerns, which gave her room to grow as a professional.

Jodi Marchesso in Pasadena USD works with some teachers who have been in the district a while and seem to be resistant to trying different instructional practices. To try to determine the cause of their hesitation, she has worked with them during student activities and assisted with their labs. Those actions have started to build trust and the teachers seem to connect with her more during PD days. According to Marchesso, "Sadly, sometimes it can take a couple of years to get into a resistant teacher's classroom or get them to sit down to talk about the changes the NGSS is going to bring to their classroom."

Implementation of the NGSS requires different instructional strategies and the use of PBLs, engineering, and technology. Marchesso knows that it is hard for the transition to occur, and perhaps there is a level of fear. It would be easiest for teachers to use what they have done before—especially when it gets tough. But to continue to be effective they will need to adopt a STEM perspective and the instructional strategies that are more inquiry-based and student-centered. She has doubled her efforts to build trust now, so she can connect with teachers, and help the STEM practices to become routine, so that when the NGSS adoption is complete, they are ready and successful.

As an astute coach, Marchesso recognizes the concerns that an experienced and veteran teacher would feel if she were unsuccessful. She knows this can occur while trying a new strategy or while working with someone in authority who is younger and/or savvier in STEM instruction. So as a result, she is working to build their trust, to create a safe environment where experimentation with strategies is expected. Her goal is to coach them through those first few missteps in implementation, and help them to see their adjustments as part of a natural progression in learning.

Teacher Talk that Reveals Concern About Change

Joe Ferrara's doctorate focused on concerns teachers have when implementing a new innovation, in this case STEM problem and project-based learning. He used the stages of concern questionnaire (SoCQ), which is one of the diagnostics dimensions of the concerns-based adoption model (CBAM), originally researched and developed by Dr. Shirley Hord et al.—see *Taking Charge Of Change* (1987).

In CBAM, Hord explains that everyone who is involved in the transition will respond in a different way. They will have their attitudes and beliefs challenged as they are asked to adopt a new way of thinking and being. Hord's model provides three diagnostics to determine where each individual is in the highly personal process. The model shows coaches how they must prepare everyone involved for the transition, provide support throughout the process, and monitor for continued implementation once the transition is complete.

Ferrara administered the SoCQ prior to teachers' professional development to determine their attitudes and beliefs about STEM PBL. He used data from the SoCQ to align professional development experiences and follow-up coaching to the needs of participants. He then followed up with a post-PD SoCQ to monitor whether teacher concerns were being met. This monitoring allowed him to target coaching and was the most effective way to achieve high levels of implementation. He concluded that by listening to their concerns and monitoring those concerns through a coaching model, he increased teacher implementation. He was able to differentiate his levels of support based on their levels of concern.

Coaching Conversations

Based on the CBAM model, a coach has an opportunity to pinpoint where a teacher is in the implementation of a new strategy or program through a short, informative conversation in passing. As outlined in *Taking Charge Of Change*, the coach can determine the interventions that might respond to teachers' concerns. Through the process a coach can assess and respond to the worries, attitudes, and perceptions of the teachers as they deal with the challenges of changing their instructional practice. The coach can determine the stage of concern about the new instructional model and adjust the scaffolding accordingly. The stages of concern are: stage 0—unconcerned; stage 1—informational concerns; stage 2—personal concerns; stage 3—management concerns; stage 4—consequences concerns; stage 5—collaborative concerns; and stage 6—refocusing concerns.

When a teacher begins a conversation with her coach, talking about how stressed she is because of trying new things, the focus is still on herself. She can't seem to manage her time or the resources well or that being organized is overwhelming. But, as a teacher becomes more comfortable or better skilled with the strategy her concerns shift to focusing on the broader impact and how it will affect students. The coach can recognize that the teacher is moving forward in her adoption of the program and has a lower level of concern and higher level of implementation.

It is when the teacher reveals a lack of awareness or the need to know more because she is not sure what is expected of her in the implementation of the program, that the coach has reason to be concerned. The CBAM model also addresses the levels of use for an innovation. Based on the same conversation, responses to coaches' questions can determine where the teacher is in implementation of the program or strategy. The levels of use are: level 0— nonuse; level 1—orientation; level 2—preparation; level 3—mechanical use; level 4a—routine; level 4b—refinement; level 5—integration; and level 6— renewal. In order to determine the effectiveness of a strategy towards student achievement it needs to be fully implemented by the teacher before a determination can be made as to the effectiveness of the instructional strategy.

Sharing Coaching Information with Administration

According to Dillon Chevalier, sometimes, out of curiosity, the principals ask for information about their teachers, but his superintendent advised the members of his STEM coaching cadre not to share their data. He warned of a potential loss of trust. Although it is hard to go without the coaches' insights, the principals know the trust that the coaches have established with their teachers might be the factor that could impact a change in instructional practices. While Chevalier was with the district there were no plans to share the observation data with anyone. It was a conversation between the coach and the teacher—one that was held in confidence.

8

The Coaching Cycle

The Complete Cycle

In Lancaster, according to Kenya Wilson, "We use two coaching sessions: one before the lesson and a reflective one after the lesson. As a coach, I observe mostly." A typical coaching session for Wilson is broken into three sections: 1) Discussion Before The Observation, 2) The Observation, and 3) Debriefing The Observation. Because it is a coaching session she uses questioning strategies to allow the teacher to reveal her thinking about the choices she considered and the ones she selected. There is a STEM lens through which both the content and the STEM standards are addressed.

In the Discussion Before The Observation, Wilson and the teacher review and discuss the lesson plans. Some of the coach's questions include:

◆ Did you teach this lesson last year? If so:
  ● What were your reflections from last year and data from students?
  ● Could you foresee how they could incorporate the information into future studies or careers? How did your students integrate the information into a pipeline track?
◆ What pipeline track is aligned to that learning?
  ● To which area of the Pipeline Track did you specifically focus this lesson?
  ● How is it aligned?
  ● What were some of the changes you made because of the data or reflection?
◆ As I observe, which data have you decided you want me to focus on?
  ● In which format would it be most valuable?

An example of a Discussion Before The Observation occurred when Wilson was coaching in ELA and the teacher wanted her students to write a proposal for a new facility. They were looking at making sure something was in place to include procedural text. The ELA core components were done but it also needed a STEM component. So, the teacher suggested relating it to the health-related careers pipeline track and wrapping in the ELA components. The students were to plan a medical facility and address how a designer would go about getting input for what it was to include. Wilson's final question for the teacher was, "How do you want to teach it differently to include the STEM focus and how well is it aligned to the pipeline objectives?" Wilson shared:

> If I am asked to model a strategy, I do so only during a portion of the lesson. I ask the teacher to take notes while I model it so we can talk afterwards about what I did and why. I only model at the start of the year. The remainder of the year I mostly just observe. After I model it, I observe them doing it and then debrief what I observed and how they felt about it. We then plan to implement it into a following lesson.

In the Observation section of the coaching session, Wilson shows up at the scheduled date and time:

> During the lesson that I am observing, whether videotaped or not, I use a checklist to observe for key routines, student and teacher actions, as well as teacher questions and student responses. I listen for those things we planned for in the pre-briefing. I also collect data on other key items to share afterwards.

The third session, Debriefing The Observation, is a reflection. It is a series of questions to reveal what the teacher's goals were for the lesson and how closely they met their goals:

◆ How do you think that went?
◆ What was your strongest point in the lesson and why do you think that?
◆ What part of the lesson do you think was your weakest and why do you think that?
◆ How would you like to follow up on weak points with that class?
◆ How can I support you? (I can send resources, model strategies, co-teach.)
◆ Set a goal for implementing one different strategy, and what will it look like?
◆ Let's set a date for the next observation and coaching cycle.

Wilson shared an example of a debriefing she did with a teacher who revealed, "I didn't have control of class during one portion of the lesson." She said next time she wanted to try a different strategy for guided practice. She shared some ideas about some cooperative learning strategies that use smaller groups and a protocol that she had read about. The teacher and Wilson discussed what some would look like and if they would add some control to the class flow. The teacher decided to try one. Wilson added, "We discussed what it would look like if it were successful and set a date for me to return."

Dr. Leslie Hancock, onsite instructional coach in GCISD, shared her three phases of the coaching cycle. Her coaching cycle starts with an initial conversation that lasts about 45 minutes. She builds rapport by asking teachers about themselves, their students, and their content and agrees upon norms for the critical conversations, which will be part of the coaching process. Hancock leads them through a set of questions, which includes some such as: "How do you define yourself as teacher, and learner, and how would you describe your mindset?" Hancock asks the teacher about what surprises them in their students and what surprises them in their classrooms. She also asks, "What makes your content unique and challenging to teach, and why did you choose that content area?"

> I avoid being critical of what and how they are teaching. I always ask questions and assume they have positive intent. For example I would ask, "How did you structure note taking for your students?" rather than asking them, "Why didn't you use or provide a structure for note taking?"

When Hancock observes a teacher, they set an agreed upon time and she films 10–15 minutes of teaching. The content of the video need not be anything special, just something for which they might like feedback. She asks that they look at the video by themselves and fill out a reflection form. When Hancock returns for the next visit, they debrief and discuss what they saw. The teacher shares what she loved and what she wanted feedback on. Then, the two look at setting goals and developing an action plan for the realization of those goals.

Hancock visits every new teacher once every two months and repeats the same cycle. The next observation can be about a new goal or the same goal. The intent is to craft it into a proof of evolution for their formal teacher evaluation.

Joe Todd has developed coaching protocols for two types of sessions that he uses as an instructional coach: one for an experienced teacher and the other for a new teacher:

I worked with an experienced teacher in the technology cadre. He was reluctant to try to use sensors or the Google classroom because it didn't fit with what he had done in the past with that unit of instruction. He is a coach and during this time of year he was pretty heavily involved with a tournament. During this crunch time, his preparation time is limited, so he made the choice to not integrate new technologies into the study of the actual phenomenon. He chose to teach the unit the way he had taught it before. He integrated technology but selected to use simulations as his way of showing the phenomena to his students. But, the simulation software was no longer available through the district and he did not feel that he had time to learn a new way to have a technology-based experience for his students. He was willing to pay for the simulation out of his own pocket.

Through this, I was able to coach and guide him to express his views about what he wanted for his students' futures—not just the future we can predict now but for the future we don't even understand as yet. He articulated that he wanted his kids to be prepared for a future that deals with actual phenomena and not simulations. We want to use technology to deeply explore the phenomenon and not just simulate it.

We discussed how hands-on activities would impact his instruction, and how did he want the learning to look? So that opened up an opportunity to briefly show him how to use an air pressure sensor and how it detects production of a gas through the use of a catalyst.

After Todd showed the teacher how to use the technology and a strategy for incorporating it into his lessons, he made it clear there was an expectation that the teacher would use both the strategy and technology with his students. The teacher hesitated and Todd suggested that he would be happy to model its use with his students as well, because they were learning together as they went along. The teacher wanted to try using the technology and strategy, but decided to delay incorporating the technology within the current instructional unit because he was busy with the tournament and could not get organized enough to do it well.

After discussion of schedules, the teacher asked to schedule with Todd a time they were both available in January, during the unit of study of respiration. Todd replied that he would be on hand to model the use of technology with his morning classes and, in the afternoon, be available to assist and support him as he teaches his students in the afternoon. "In this way, I was able to build capacity in this teacher as he took on more of the instruction throughout the day."

Todd chose to use a different coaching model when working with a new middle school teacher. The novice teacher had been directed by his department chair to "take come compounds and list them on the board; and then demonstrate combining them in front of the class." After the demonstration the students were to do Internet research to find out why the combinations reacted in certain ways. The final portion of the described lesson included students working in lab groups and doing experiments to determine if they were right or wrong:

> I had to bite my tongue because I was familiar with this lab and knew it was an injustice for the kids to not have an inquiry experience with it directly. I modeled it for him using an inquiry approach, with temperature sensors and he chose to do it that way.

Todd stayed with the teacher the next period and observed. The teacher did it as he was directed and he had his kids use sensors. Todd was there to support him third period, fourth period, and the rest of the day. Later in the week, Todd returned to the campus and checked in with him. The students' content retention was consistently strong; they displayed their understanding when they had the opportunity to interact with the materials in the lab.

Todd, as an instructional coach, made the choice to use a coaching model with the experienced teacher who was seeking a way to integrate a new type of technology into his already STEM-based program. Through Todd's questioning strategy, he was able to help the teacher clarify his thinking about the types and purposes of the available technology he could use and to select one that was more hands-on, engaging, and inquiry-based.

When working with the novice teacher who was unaware of the possibility of using technology in an authentic way to make accurate observations about the changes occurring during chemical reactions, Todd was able to provide an intervention that made a demonstration become interactive and engaging through suggesting the use of technology. Did you notice the subtle difference? Rather than asking questions about his thinking and choices, Todd made suggestions for ways to make the lesson inquiry-based, engaging, and interactive through the use of technology; he also provided advice in the ways to ask the facilitating questions that generated curiosity and interest in the students.

The most effective professional development can be the time spent one-on-one with an instructional coach, who is knowledgeable, has expertise, and who understands the developmental levels in content knowledge and instructional strategies of those he is coaching. Kathryn Kee, an International Coach Federation professional certified coach, shares her insights about using the language of a coach in *Saying It Like a Coach* (2006). Her insights provide a backdrop for using "skilled language and an intention to support educators as they modify and adjust to potentially new strategies [which] becomes a dance of building rapport and trust while communicating respect for where a teacher is or has been while on the journey to new and promising practices."

Kee is one of the authors of *Results Coaching, The New Essential for School Leaders* (2010) along with her colleagues Karen Anderson, Vicky Dearing, Edna Harris, and Frances Shuster. The leadership provided by this team of coaches has influenced many of the coaches highlighted in this book. The mnemonic RESULTS is a scaffold utilized in *Results Coaching*. It is the navigation system that impacts new thinking and finding solutions. RESULTS focuses on clarifying goals, investigating multiple solution options, and building new pathways in the brain for thinking that moves people to action. According to Kee et al.,

> The model accelerates deep thinking and unleashes multiple ways to succeed. Quite simply it is as follows:
>
> R...Resolve to change results
> E...Establish goal clarity
> S...Seek integrity
> U...Unveil multiple pathways
> L...Leverage options
> T...Take Action
> S...Seize success

Based on the RESULTS model, coaches as instructional leaders are valuable in fostering continuous growth and improvement in the teachers they serve, by first using the language of a coach that does not advise, but seeks to be the agent for thinking more deeply about teachers' instructional practice. Coaches impact all aspects of teaching and learning. Coaching with the intentional language of a coach will build trust, confidence, and competence through open and reflective conversations.

Lesson Planning in PLCs

Professional learning communities (PLCs) are teacher/learners who meet as a group and are led by an instructional coach, who is the facilitator. PLCs are an opportunity for teachers to engage in collaborative lesson-planning sessions. This is an opportunity for professional educators to join forces to tackle an instructional challenge. The discourse and intellectual exchanges lead not only to high-quality instructional materials and assessments, but also to a new understanding about the impact of good instructional practices on student work and gains in student achievement.

The positive impact on the levels of thinking that occur while engaged in collaborative lesson planning sessions is supported in education research. Not only is the quality and depth of teachers' thinking enhanced, so are the cognitive challenges for students, which result in increased academic achievement for the students. For lesson plans and resources to be aligned to the standards and to meet the differentiated needs of all students, teachers need to gain a deeper understanding of the content standards. It is through facilitated discussions led by the STEM instructional coach that mastery learning for all students is possible. The coach's expertise and experience in breaking down the standards, integrating learning across content boundaries, and using effective instructional strategies helps make the lessons engaging, inquiry-based, and learner-centered; all benefit. Teachers learn from and with each other.

In the opinion of Jodi Marchesso, new teachers and those who are new to STEM want to spend most of their coaching time lesson planning. Although there is great value in that for the novice, there is greater value in novice teachers planning with their PLC groups.

A 2015 research study by Ronfeldt, Farmer, McQueen, and Grissom published in the *American Educational Research Journal* shows that, on average, teachers and schools that engage in better quality collaboration have better achievement gains in math and reading. In addition, teachers improve at greater rates when they work in schools with better collaboration quality. In the study the authors investigated in which area of planning the impact was the greatest, focusing on the three areas about curriculum and instructional strategies, students, or assessments.

The results showed that collaborative planning for curriculum and instructional strategies saw the most gains when planning included coordinating curriculum across classrooms, developing the instructional strategies, and developing aligned materials. In the second area, students, the most gains were found when collaborative planning included the needs of specific students, reviewing student work, and addressing classroom management issues. In the final area, the most gains made through collaboration were from reviewing state test results and planning formative assessments.

If the findings of the study can be applied to the coaching relationship, collaboration in the design of lessons would have a positive impact on student achievement. Sharry Whitney used PLCs as a way to provide collaboration:

I chose to set up PLCs where teachers met with other teachers as a team. I acted as a facilitator. I knew from my observations and analysis of student data what they were struggling with. But as facilitator, I developed a way to lead the conversation in such a way that they began to share their common struggles. I crunched the numbers, brought them research-based resources, and provided a span of time for them to discuss their needs and ideas. As a professional learning community they decided what the best things would be for their students.

Marisa Guzman, the science–math coach in Katy ISD, facilitates professional learning communities (PLCs) as lesson-planning sessions. During the weekly PLC session members of the team have conversations about their upcoming lessons, resources they have and the needs of their students that may require some modifications to the shared documents. They also analyze data from past lessons and to find out what is happening. They may make decisions to reteach as needed. They discuss struggling students and ways to keep the strong students growing.

Guzman knows the data are needed to drive the decisions the PLC will make towards how they will address student achievement and bounce ideas off each other and her. She is always prepared for new ideas and they respect her for that. The data come from assessments and looking at student work.

From the perspective of K-12 STEM coach Denise Fisher, planning lessons during PLCs is a means to keep the STEM lens focused on the selection of highly effective instructional strategies and respectful student work. Alignment to the state standards and the STEM objectives of the *T-STEM Design Blueprint* requires the development of cross-curricular units that are based on the content of the standards taught with highly effective instructional strategies focused in STEM practices. She works from a belief that, by keeping the engineering design process in the forefront of planning sessions, the STEM culture of the district begins to emerge.

In Fisher's opinion, the engineering design process is used to systematically solve problems and needs to be part of all planning. Students use technology-based authentic sources to do research, then imagine, brainstorm, plan, design, and build their prototype. Materials are selected within the given constraints of time and budget. Through a STEM-based approach to science and math instruction, student engagement and interest is high. They seek deeper scientific understanding to evaluate their decisions and make choices. They develop a need to understand the functions of mathematics as they make decisions about the benefits or liabilities of the resources available within constraints of a budget and time. When presenting their prototypes, as a team of engineers, they are able to explain using the deeper understanding of science concepts and math processes. Learning of these concepts is evident in the sophisticated solutions that have been designed and presented.

When the focus is on student learning and teachers continually learning, the STEM coach as a facilitator keeps the planning on target. The coach uses the collaboration process to deepen the thinking, engage in discourse about student learning, and create expertise among those engaged in the process. Teachers are empowered to design systems that make achievement possible and pull from the resources of the group.

In their 2008 study published in the journal *Teaching and Teacher Education* Vescio and Adams report that of all the factors that impact student achievement in reading, writing, math, science, and social studies, PLCs had a positive effect. The four characteristics identified by the study that were inherent in PLCs are collaboration, a focus on student learning, teacher authority, and continual teacher learning.

Observing a Lesson

There are four situations when teacher observations usually occur on a campus. The most common is the annual teacher evaluation when the principal sits in a teacher's classroom for the full period and evaluates the teacher's proficiency based on a rubric or checklist. It is for evaluation and required by the district and often the state education agency. It may or may not have a series of "walk-through" observations associated with it. These shorter observations can be added to the body of evidence about the proficiency of the teacher. The evaluation observation is usually preceded with a brief meeting to set up the date and review the criteria and is concluded with another short meeting with the observer to go over the results and sign the paperwork.

The second type of observation is non-evaluative, but instructional. It occurs when a mentor teacher accompanies a novice teacher to observe a master teacher conducting a lesson; it is usually prearranged for date and time beforehand. Often there is much to gain when a novice teacher not only observes but also has an opportunity to process everything they noticed with their mentor. It is important for the mentor to accompany the new teacher for the observation: to point out strategic behaviors, to bring attention to the instructional strategies, and to highlight classroom management techniques used that are occurring as the lesson unfolds.

A novice teacher may not notice or understand how the smoothness of transitions and flow of the lesson are maintained. The mentor is there to point out the subtle teacher actions that happen and the students' responses to them. The mentor and novice teacher follow up outside the classroom by discussing the conscious decisions the master teacher made in the moment. They also discuss the established routines that made the facilitation seamless. Often this is followed up with a thank you note to the master teacher.

The third type of observation is also non-evaluative and provides an opportunity for the STEM coach and principal to focus on the integration of STEM strategies and student engagement levels at various times in the lesson cycle. These observations are usually five to ten minutes in length and are focused on what is happening at the time. The common name for these observations is a "walk-through" because the observers do not sit down, nor do they see the entire lesson cycle. After observing the interactions between students and teachers the principal and STEM coach step into the hallway and calibrate what they have seen.

This is a highly effective learning opportunity for campus leadership. Just as with the novice teacher, observing for the effective instructional practices that have been part of PLC discussions, professional development sessions, and mentoring and coaching interactions lets the teachers know how much value campus leadership places on the STEM practices. It also helps the principal to recognize the levels of use of the desired teacher behaviors associated with district and campus initiatives. This is usually followed up by leaving my business card with a note on the back. I place it on the teacher's desk or in their mailbox. My note usually says, "Thank you for allowing us to watch your students in action!"

The last type of observation is also non-evaluative and part of a coaching cycle. As a coach I observe for several specific things and also collect data based on what we discussed in our first session. I stay for the entire period and observe for the following specific teacher behaviors:

◆ Is the learning target posted in student language?
◆ Do the students know how the target will be assessed at the end of instruction?
◆ Are students actively engaged in learning and asking questions?
◆ Has the teacher divided the learning into manageable chunks?
◆ Is there more purposeful student talk than teacher talk?
◆ Has the teacher checked for understanding?
◆ Are there artifacts of learning in the room?
◆ Is there evidence of technology integration?
◆ Are career connections being made?

During this time I script student-and-teacher interactions as well as student-to-student interactions. I also tally the number and types of questions asked by the teacher and if wait time is utilized. I will not share all this information with the teacher, but it allows me to track their progress. This data will be used for the debrief part of the coaching session.

Using an Observation Protocol or Checklist

Key to an observation being usable by the teacher to grow in STEM craft knowledge, content skills, and instructional strategies, is the importance that the observation criteria used are linked to effective practices that impact student engagement and achievement. The evaluation rubric may not have criteria for STEM practices, and if not observed for, teachers are given the false impression that they are not valued.

Key to effective observations of STEM-centered classrooms is an understanding of how a STEM-based classroom culture differs from that of a traditional classroom. An observation protocol or shorter checklist of the best practices for constructivist learning and student-centered instruction should be constructed and used for each observation. If STEM practices such as cooperative learning, project-based learning, engineering design, purposeful student talk, hands-on learning, authentic scientific and engineering practices, career connections, and technology integration are not part of the observation criteria, the data analysis and feedback for teacher growth in STEM are not possible.

An observation protocol lists key instructional practices and habits of mind that are to be observed. These are further broken down into indicators that fine-tuned the practice. For each of the indicators the criteria that describe the increasing levels of proficiency from beginner to expert teacher are listed. The value of a growth rubric such as this is that when shared with the teacher, they know how they can change the caliber of their practice through gaining more skill and practicing specifically based on the indicator and criteria. Observation checklists do not contain the indicators or criteria; they just lists the behaviors, and provide a place for notes for evidence or data. Checklists work best for walk-through observations rather than a full class period observation.

A 2012 report by Darling-Hammond for the Stanford Center for Opportunity Policy in Education identifies five key features of effective teacher evaluation systems that also support effective teaching: 1) start with standards, 2) create performance-based assessments, 3) build a standards-based system of local evaluation, 4) create structures to support high-quality, fair, and effective evaluation, and 5) create aligned professional-learning opportunities. The report also reviews the evidence discouraging the use of value-added modeling in teacher evaluation practices.

Using Videos to Support Thinking About STEM Practices

Asking teachers to video themselves can be stressful. Depending on their personality and learning style, it can help or get in the way. STEM instructional coach Kenya Wilson usually doesn't record the lesson. But, for those that she does video, she asks them to watch their video by themselves and write a reflection. She asks them to watch it several times and then select one or two small portions that they can watch together on her next visit. The criteria for the selection of the clips are that they need to be ones they want to work on. She never takes the videos with her. Wilson downloads it to their computer and teachers watch it by themselves.

She also never shares the videos. It is theirs and she feels that she would be breaking their trust if she shared it. Wilson states:

> For teachers who are struggling, during the observation I look for 3 things to work on. I usually select the one that is most urgent to correct by tomorrow. For these observations I will frequently video the session to get counts for data. I count proximity, random questions, or use of multiple strategies. I tally the number of times the teacher used each strategy and how the students respond. The video helps me to be accurate and so we can also document improvements.

Dr. Joe Ferrara stated that his main focus when he developed his coaching model was to assist teachers in helping themselves. He chose to build teacher capacity and help teachers recognize what quality instructional practice looked like. He said, "They don't need me here for 10 years to continue to coach them on the same things. We need to build and support teacher capacity through appropriate PD, practical experiences, and resources that are aligned to these experiences."

Ferrara believes teachers build capacity by seeing how they teach, identifying opportunities to change their practice, and then selecting the appropriate strategies to improve that practice. Many coaching models use videos to assist in the coaching process. Ferrara says, "In my experience, teachers become very stressed when you even mention watching a video with them. As a result, I moved away from the viewing of videos with teachers unless they ask me to." In his coaching model, teachers utilize a device called a Swivl. Teachers place a smart phone or tablet in the Swivl and wear a device around their neck that connects with the Swivl via Bluetooth. As the teacher walks around the room the camera follows and records all video and audio, capturing the full instructional experience.

Afterwards, the teacher views their video on their own using checklists to guide their analysis. The checklists contains specific behaviors associated with instructional strategies such as facilitating PBL activities or managing student behavior. Checklists are also available to look at student behavior. The teacher chooses the checklist based on the element they wish to focus on. Results are shared with the coach, who can then assist in selecting the appropriate strategy or resources to address that element:

> I usually never see their video until they feel great about their practice. That is an awesome experience for a coach. The purpose is to coach themselves and seek resources. Once they can do this, we can move on to other things.

9

Other Ways to Provide Feedback

Teachers who are skillful in their craft and are seeking to become master teachers in STEM often want other forms of feedback to support their efforts towards increasing student achievement. The STEM coach and instructional coaches can provide additional information to inform teachers about where change is needed by analyzing data obtained by tracking interactions during an observation, disaggregated data from assessments, and evaluating student work. Inquiry about trends in data from all sources can be discussed in collaborative groups such as professional learning communities (PLCs), where teachers can gain insight on a broader, more global scale than just for their classroom.

Tracking Observation Data

As a STEM coach, I found it helpful for some teachers to have me draw out a classroom map on a blank sheet of paper. I would draw their path as they moved about the room during a lesson. I would mark teacher–student interactions, student–student interactions, and tally questions. Often such data were useful when asking teachers to reflect on student responses to their questions and the frequency of each student's responses to questions. I would find that most new teachers do not realize they are not calling on students equally, or that they are asking the same students over and over again, because they know they will get the correct answer when they are called on. Often when teaching, little attention is paid to equity of questions asked of each student and the levels of the questions. Tallying questions and responses provides data for working towards mastery of strategies surrounding questions and equal voice.

As a coach when setting goals for the next observation, we would work through ways to increase the rigor of questions, the ways to allow for student collaboration in formulating responses, using teacher proximity for encouraging reluctant students to respond, and ensuring all students have equity in the opportunity to respond to questions and the amount of time given for their response before calling on another student.

Analyzing Data from Assessments

With the use of technology aids such as electronically read answer sheets, online testing, and scanned answer documents many of the curriculum-based assessments can be scored and the scores aggregated if they are in a multiple-choice format. The data can then be placed in spreadsheets for analysis. Some teachers enjoy the efforts in doing that for their test scores; others find no interest in it at all. Most teachers find they are data rich, but time poor and cannot spend the time disaggregating all the data for their students.

As a STEM or instructional coach, you have an opportunity to determine the trends district wide. Student responses to test items can be analyzed for several alignment factors: to content standards, to the curriculum, and of the resources to the standards. Teachers get a clearer picture of where to focus their attention and possibly enrich the curriculum when this information is provided in a timely, effective, and non-threatening manner.

There are many useful ways to disaggregate assessment data and share results with teachers. Through district data analysis packages, coaches can provide teachers with charts that are suited to this type of analysis. So the data are not overwhelming or pointing towards specific teachers, it is essential to establish norms of behavior before the data being presented. Data alone will not improve instruction. It is through the analysis for gaps in instruction and resource alignment that curriculum and instruction can be adjusted to meet the needs of the students for content mastery.

Evaluating Student Work

One of the most successful applications of data analysis comes from looking at student work. When in a PLC setting anonymous student writing samples are compared for levels of thinking and accuracy of science content, teachers can collaboratively make some suggestions for ways to differentiate instruction to meet the needs of the learners. Although not all student work is shared, when each teacher submits a sample of low-, medium-, and high-level student work there are enough samples to begin to see trends in skills, misconceptions, and gaps in the curriculum in addressing the content.

In a large study published in the *Journal of Research in Science Teaching* (2012), Heller et al. find that, among the three teacher interventions employed—teaching cases, looking at student work, and metacognitive analysis—teaching cases and looking at student work improved the accuracy and completeness of students' written justifications of test answers.

10

Roadblocks to Coaching

How to Recognize They're Stuck

According to Janelle McLaughlin, there are probably two roadblocks that keep coaching from being successful. When being asked to try something new, some teachers will tell you it is about the time. There isn't enough time for the change. But, in McLaughlin's opinion, it is a fear of trying new things. Maybe it is a mix of both. Fortunately, with the coaching McLaughlin is doing in technology, many of the teachers she works with have the choice of opting in:

> They want to be doing this. As a curriculum director I found many teachers did not want to change or try new things for a number of reasons. Many saw themselves as the experts in their content area and thought I had nothing they needed for their content. My perspective is always that I am here to make your job better or easier. Let's work together to make it better.

> When it comes to technology, many are afraid that they are being evaluated on their use of technology. They do not want to be evaluated on their growth pathway. They knew they would stumble along the way and not be successful at first. They were cautious about their failures being exposed. Perhaps we as coaches overlook those complex thoughts.

Getting Unstuck

To help teachers to overcome these roadblocks, McLaughlin highlights their strengths. She doesn't have a long relationship with each teacher she coaches since they don't meet on a daily basis. When in a one-on-one session she provides lots of encouragement and praise for their efforts. "You are already doing it! You did this successfully as well, now let's add to that." She breaks each process down into achievable action steps to break through:

> To overcome their fear of being evaluated while they were still learning, I talked with district leadership through follow up communication. I let them know this is what I saw, the progress being made, and make recommendations for follow up. I emphasize that we encourage a risk-taking environment and request that they do not tie this learning process to the evaluations of their teachers. In the end, to keep teachers motivated and willing to be coached, it all comes back to relationship building, with the leadership team and then with the faculty. Positive relationships trickle down through the entire faculty.

Felecia Pittman, T-STEM coach, found there were several roadblocks that slowed implementation of the state STEM initiatives and stopped them moving forward at the campus and district levels. Some of the more common roadblocks included a lack of a foundation of support from the district administration and a lack of capacity. Often times the lack of capacity was within the campus leadership because the responsibility for implementation fell to one person who was to drive the STEM initiative. Sometimes the campus faculty as a whole was not invested in it. On other campuses this was not the case, but most often the implementation of the STEM initiative was in the hands of just one person. Pittman felt that, "If he or she left the campus, the STEM initiative would lose momentum. To have to start over again, implementation would be even more difficult due to trying to get others involved."

In Lancaster ISD as a district-level team, they kept their eyes on data, campus performance reviews and looking at the current status of student achievement. Sometimes coaches will acknowledge areas where they have encountered resistance from teachers. When coaches feel they are not making progress, they discuss the situation with the chief academic officer or principal of the campus. In these fierce conversations they discuss what the coaches understand to be the campus initiatives for implementation and what they are seeing in the classroom. The discussion becomes focused on what everyone wants to see. It is through these fierce conversations that they develop a plan for coaching to change behaviors and teacher actions that are engaging and impact student achievement. There is also an agreement that the campus leader will monitor the changes.

For Dr. Ferrara, an experienced instructional coach in the Dallas-Ft Worth, TX, ISD and currently director at the UTD Institute for Instructional Excellence, the main roadblock to coaching was around assigned duties that were not directly related to the role of the coach. In his opinion, "You can't have a coach assigned to the building who doesn't spend the majority of their time doing coaching activities. This results in drive by coaching, which is a waste of resources, and feeds teacher resentment."

Time maps and time logs help you assess how much time is actually spent coaching. At one time, only 38% of Ferrara's time was spent actually coaching teachers. Other things got in the way, such as writing benchmark assessments and reviewing campus improvement plans for non-instructional purposes. "If coaching is to be successful, it has to be valued and respected by leadership as an effective tool to increase teacher capacity and student achievement."

Dr. Leslie Hansen, in GCISD, believes that, for many teachers, the biggest obstacle is their mindset. Some people perceive working with a coach to be indicative of a deficit in practice. "But that is not so; if you are growth minded you want to further your practice. I'm in the business of educating and growing learners and teachers."

Kyndra Johnson's roadblocks were too few instructional coaches for the number of teachers they served. Their role as coaches included being resource managers and curriculum developers, which did not allow much time in the classrooms supporting teachers.

11

The STEM Coaches and Professional Development

Administration Professional Learning

In Lancaster ISD, Kyndra Johnson shared the district's vision and two goals for each campus: the goal for STEM implementation and the goal for higher student achievement. Johnson saw the two goals as working simultaneously in preparing students for their futures. Through data-driven conversations with the campus leaders, Johnson gained an understanding of the unique needs of each campus as they addressed student learning, achievement, and STEM implementation. Using student achievement data was not about playing "got-cha" but was about knowing the kinds of supports each campus needs. The conversations built a strong bond between the district and the campuses.

In Texarkana ISD, Denise Fisher, STEM coordinator and K-12 STEM coach, learned that to coach an administrator in STEM is sometimes like walking a tightrope. It is hard to maintain a perspective on the balance needed between initiatives for student achievement gains and the district's initiative for the infusion of STEM strategies and student engagement. Fisher stated that some principals are open and allowed the coaches to set the targets and expectations when it was about the STEM curriculum:

> But, others are not as open. They are only focused on the initiatives for student achievement and filtered all other initiatives through that lens. Although they know other initiatives are important, they are driven by how their campus will be judged by test scores.

In both situations, they as coaches knew that they could not achieve their targets without a high-quality curriculum, good instructional practices, alignment of instruction to assessments, and focus on the qualities of a well-rounded, successful graduate from their programs. Principals may not have the time to know and do everything that needs to be done for the instructional program on their campuses. Often they may not have the knowledge or skill set to go about setting it up and maintaining it.

It was the role of the Texarkana's STEM instructional team to support principals through a partnership. They partnered for developing knowledge and skills in the integration of STEM-based, quality instructional programs for their students, staff, campus leadership team, and themselves. As teachers and administrators began to trust the STEM instructional team, principals began to realize the STEM focus could fulfill their goals. The STEM initiatives provided the rich instructional climate needed on their campuses for increased student achievement to be possible. As an instructional team, Fisher's team understood that the development of a deep understanding of STEM-based strategies is along a continuum towards the Big Picture. According to Fisher,

> As Chip and Dan Heath, in their book *Switch* (2010) called it, "the picture postcard." That is the picture of our final destination, the beautiful and peaceful place, where we want our campuses and graduates to be at the end of our journey.

Their first steps were to set up professional learning for principals in a safe, learning environment where they could let down their guard, take risks, have discourse, and collaborate with their peers for planning and implementing best practices for their students' and teachers' success. Based on gaining an understanding of STEM programs they know the "what" and the "why": what STEM looks like and the value of an integrated STEM-based program. They became prepared to watch and look for STEM integration and instructional strategies in the classrooms on their campuses. They also worked through how to hold teachers accountable for their efforts in making STEM part of the everyday routines in their classrooms.

As principals began to observe for STEM integration, coaches would accompany them on "learning walks." Coaches helped the principals to pick out the subtle changes that occur when there is a STEM focus in the classroom. The coaches talked about what it should look like, what they wanted to see in the way of instructional strategies, and the culture and climate of a learning-centered classroom. It was beneficial to coach about the little things that popped up as they were observing and they were able to think through how to follow up in the moment.

As principals and STEM coaches observe teachers engaged in instructing students, often what is not observed is as important as what is observed. For example, teachers may miss an opportunity to integrate STEM ideas and strategies such as a career connection comment while engaging in a PBL. Providing in-the-moment feedback to a teacher about a missed instructional opportunity can be powerful in changing their future instructional practice. The benefits of being there to coach principals during learning walks were the opportunity to reveal and discuss the fine lines between a STEM and non-STEM focus; what it looks like and what it doesn't.

Often, the Texarkana principals used the cadre of STEM coaches to help them understand what to do as teachers pushed back. They heard their teachers complain and vocalize how uncomfortable they were with the changes that were occurring, and when their former routines were being challenged. Principals were asked to justify why they allowed coaches the right to examine the usefulness of long-held instructional practices that had been successful in the past. Why were these strategies now being questioned, adapted, or abandoned? Teachers complained about the lack of time to add one more thing to their already crowded syllabus. They worried about decreasing the time spent on test preparation without the guarantee of high tests scores. By understanding STEM and having a deeper knowledge of STEM instructional practices, principals who already understood the why, and the how, were now able to support their teachers, to motivate and assure them that the destination is worth the effort.

As with all growth processes, it is important not to judge teachers by the failures they encounter as they try new strategies. Sharing a teacher's successful implementation of STEM or a new instructional strategy with the principal is important and, just as important, is keeping the principal apprised of the progress being made. The principals, through their walk-through protocols, are observing for changes and rating them. But it is of utmost importance that teachers are not judged on their unpolished attempts at new strategies.

The value of having STEM coaches as partners for the principals' initiatives is that principals are able to count on the coaches to support their teachers—being available as their teachers are practicing the new STEM-based strategies and gaining skills towards their proficiency and their students' increased growth. Principals need to assure teachers that each annual evaluation and walk-through would not be influenced by the failures they are observing as teachers practice their new skills and grow from their failures. As long as they are reflective in their practice, and plan for growth through these attempts, these missteps are acceptable. Principals need to let their teachers know that practicing skills for increased proficiency is their expectation: the campus leadership team is expecting to see growth in each teacher, and a lack of effort towards growth will not be accepted.

According to Denise Fisher in Texarkana there was a strong partnership between the district STEM team and the principals. Campus and district leaders partnered with her for a presentation about the district's successful STEM integration in an invited presentation for the National Research Council and National Academy of Engineering in Washington, DC:

> For one principal, I wrote the portion of the presentation for his campus and collaborated with him as he wrote the script about how coaching helped to make integrated STEM successful on his campus. He was really open to collaboration and allowed me to respond to some questions as well. Another principal was not as open and wanted the spotlight all on him as he shared his campus' successful STEM initiatives. In my mind that was OK, we were a team. It was wonderful to see how we had come together to celebrate the journey for their campuses and for their students.

Teacher Professional Learning

Lesson Studies

Among the many professional learning opportunities for STEM teachers, doing lesson studies can be one of the most beneficial. As teachers work in a collaborative session to design a lesson, they take turns observing each other as they teach the lesson. The practice has a long history in Japan and it is correlated to improving teaching and learning in the classroom: M. Yoshida outlines the process in a paper presented at the 2002 Lesson Study Conference.

Book Studies, Articles, and Blogs

The teacher that is interested in the trends and resources for STEM education need look no further than the Internet. Networks such as Facebook, Twitter, LinkedIn, and Google have groups with similar interests in STEM. The forums and blogs are rich in ideas, strategies, and case studies by familiar authors in STEM education as well as those who are dipping their toes into the STEM pool and are intrigued! Many of the resources and interviews for this book were generated by responses from the STEM groups I communicate with.

There are many websites distributing books that focus on STEM, PBLs, engineering design challenges, and others focusing on changing mindsets for the challenges that students of today will face in their lives after graduation.

Online Learning

Having a STEM teaching endorsement with your college degree in a STEM field is seen as a benefit for recent college graduates. College, university, and other STEM organizations, such as the NASA Endeavor STEM Teaching Certificate Project, are available online and are gaining popularity as a way to get a master's degree in STEM. Many of these courses require participants to provide evidence of implementation of STEM instructional practices in order to get certification. As more funding becomes available through the Federal grants focused on STEM education, an endorsement in STEM may increase employment opportunities for many generalists.

Conferences

There are several reasons a campus leader may choose to support STEM teachers' participation in off-campus professional development through conferences promoting innovation in STEM, PD sessions and workshops, or other training. This is true even after taking into consideration the sacrifice in student learning if they do not receive the same caliber of instruction through a substitute teacher, or the funds required for travel and registration expenses are taken from a limited budget. Campus leaders make the decision based on the needs of the students in the teacher's classroom and campus goals. The benefits of STEM teachers participating in off-campus professional development are found in the ideas, knowledge, and skills brought back to the campus. If implemented, those ideas will move the district and campus initiatives closer to meeting their goals.

Campuses that have recently adopted a STEM approach to learning are at the cutting edge of innovation in educational practice. With the introduction of the K-12 Framework for Science Education and the release of the NGSS many resources are now available which should be evaluated. Conferences have presentations and exhibitors, and allow for previewing many resources in one location very efficiently. Attendance at STEM-related conferences also allows for networking with others in the same roles who are evaluating resources for the same purposes.

Conferences that provide all types of resources can be found at many levels, from local and state education groups and organizations, to national and international professional organizations. National organizations such as the National Science Teachers Association (NSTA) and the National Council of Teachers of Mathematics (NCTM) hold annual and regional conferences where many presentations focus on STEM content connections. Teacher organizations at the state level also sponsor conferences, which support new ways of integrating STEM into their content areas. Organizations such as the Science Teachers Association of Texas (STAT) sponsor the annual Conference for the Advancement of Science Teaching, better known as CAST, which draws over 8,000 participants annually. More than a third of the conference sessions and vendors in the expansive exhibition area focus on ways to bring science into the 21st Century through strategies that are STEM focused.

Additionally, many universities, museums, education organizations, and publishers provide one-day to week-long sessions, workshops, and institutes where participants focus on one type of instructional strategy such as project based learning, or engineering-based strategies for use in the STEM classroom. These types of PD are more expensive and require extensive planning for teachers to be out of their classrooms. Often the added burden of days off-campus is worth the benefits of deeper learning and the greater likelihood the new learning will be implemented into classroom instruction.

Virtual Conferences and Workshops

As I was searching online for STEM coaches, Cindy Rubin contacted me. Through our messaging I found out that as a STEM-based technology coach Rubin collaborates with groups of technology coaches who have common dilemmas. She is a former high school teacher at a STEM campus in the greater Boston area. Using her expertise from education, she facilitates virtual meetings, made up of STEM technology coaches. By coaching each other in ways to solve technology integration issues about new software components or in using the components the districts have provided, they find ways to enhance STEM education. She was supporting them as they were supporting their campuses.

Rubin states that smaller districts and STEM academies often have teachers who want to integrate software but do not have the support, or who are alone in their search for solutions. Rubin became the facilitator for a group of coaches who are trying to solve problems for the success of the teachers they are serving. "As a teacher," she muses, "when you coach other teachers you become a grass roots organization." They meet via Skype or Google Hangout, coaching each other on different classes that they are instructing. When one of them runs into problems related to the technology they are using, they coach each other. Rubin pulls them together weekly and facilitates addressing their list of concerns. Everyone contributes evenly. It always has to do with integration of technology in the classroom and how to best utilize the systems the teachers have for maximum usefulness to the lesson. As a professional learning community (PLC) they are identifying and solving problems together.

Rubin as the moderator runs the agenda, listens to other people's issues as they collaborate, and ensures the group works through all suggestions. At times she contributes suggestions as well. The structure of the PLC has someone taking minutes so they can reference the minutes, make comments, and send them out to others in the group who could not attend.

As a STEM curriculum writer and consultant, Rubin finds the need to adjust what she is planning to the learning needs of the group she is presenting it to. She integrates the appropriate technology according to the grade and age group and the learning goal. "I was writing computer science curriculum when I was at the high school. I was exploring computer science curriculum, through MIT media lab, many other programs, game development and web design."

To stay current Rubin participates in many seminars and reaches out to those in the community who know more than she does. She has experience in business and looks to this sector for help as well. She invites businesses to join the network to help educators with similar issues. She advises, "A lot of people who are out in your network will connect with you. Sign up for professional development and coursework online so that you can have a rich background for your students."

Part II

Summary, Conclusion, and Resources

Being a STEM coach is a relatively new role in the education community. Instructional coaching has become more popular as the potential impact of a master teacher who acts as a campus coach becomes recognized and appears in education research. To be an effective coach the skills needed are more than for those who are considered a master teacher in their one content area, or being the most experienced on the campus.

An effective coach is one who is able to have those powerful conversations with an educator built on a relationship of trust, to bring about a commitment to change their instructional practice, for the achievement gains of their students through a lens of being college and career ready. Coaching goals include being purposeful and thoughtful in planning for coaching, and taking the steps to:

◆ Establish a relationship
◆ Use an effective coaching cycle
◆ Lead impactful professional learning communities
◆ Provide a diverse selection of professional learning opportunities
◆ Be a vehicle for reflection and growth.

The transition into a STEM campus requires a series of steps taken with the portrait of a STEM graduate in mind. The portrait is of one who is college and career ready with a view of the world through the lens of STEM. A learning environment that invites exploration, missteps, and growth that comes from authentic problem-solving and designing solutions is required. The careful development of this learning environment, which is student-centered and nurtures creativity and an open mindset, is just the beginning. Part III provides some insights and resources as you consider your plan of action.

Resources

References

Achieve, Inc. (2013). *Next Generation Science Standards* (NGSS). Washington, DC: National Academies Press.

Darling-Hammond, Linda (2012). *Creating a Comprehensive System for Evaluating and Supporting Effective Teaching*. Stanford Center for Opportunity Policy in Education, www.smmcta.com/uploads/9/9/4/2/9942134/evaluation_research_stanford_2012.pdf

Heath, Chip and Heath, Dan (2010). *Switch: How to Change Things When Change Is Hard*. New York: Broadway Books.

Heller, Joan I., Daehler, Kirsten R., Wong, Nicole, Shinohara, Mayumi, and Miratrix, Luke W. (2012). Differential Effects of Three Professional Development Models on Teacher Knowledge and Student Achievement, *Journal of Research in Science Teaching*, 49(3), 333–362, https://www.researchgate.net/publication/259129061

Hord, Shirley M., Rutherford, William L., Huling-Austin, Leslie, Hall, Gene E., and Knoll, Marcia Kalb (1987; revd 2006). *Taking Charge of Change*. Alexandria, VA: ASCD.

Ingersoll, Richard and Strong, Michael (2011). The Impact of Induction and Mentoring Programs for Beginning Teachers: A Critical Review of the Research, *Review of Education Research*, 81(2), 201–233, http://repository.upenn.edu/cgi/viewcontent.cgi?article=1127&context=gse_pubs

Kee, Kathryn (2006). Saying It Like a Coach, *National Staff Development Publication*, (November), https://coachingiu17.wikispaces.com/file/view/Say+It+Like+a+Coach+NSDC+Kathy+Kee.pdf

Ronfeldt, Matthew, Farmer, Susan Owen, McQueen, Kiel, and Grissom, Jason A. (2015). Teacher Collaboration in Instructional Teams and Student Achievement, *American Educational Research Journal*, 52(3), 475–514, http://aer.sagepub.com/content/52/3/475.full.pdf+html

Vescio, Vicki, Ross, Dorene, and Adams, Alyson (2008). A Review of Research on the Impact of Professional Learning Communities on Teaching Practice and Student Learning, *Teaching and Teacher Education*, 24(1), 80–91, http://www.k12.wa.us/Compensation/pubdocs/Vescio2008PLC-paper.pdf

Yoshida, M. (2002). Overview of Lesson Study in Japan, presented at Lesson Study Conference, www.rbs.org/SiteData/docs/yoshidaoverview/aeafddf638d3bd67526570d5b4889ae0/yoshidaoverview.pdf

Organization Websites

NASA Endeavor STEM Teaching Certificate Project—www.us-statellite.net/endeavor/
National Council of Teachers of Mathematics (NCTM)—www.nctm.org
National Science Teachers Association (NSTA)—www.nsta.org

Science Teachers Association of Texas (STAT)—www.statweb.org
Southwest Educational Development Lab (SEDL)—www.sedl.org/cbam/

Author's Recommendations

Although not cited in the chapters of Part II, the books listed above are ones that I have read while learning about how to become a better STEM coach. Friends and colleagues recommended many and some were purchased because I heard the author discuss their views and I wanted to learn more. I hope they become a source of information for you.

In her 2013 book, *The Art of Coaching: Effective Strategies for School Transformation*, Elena Aguilara suggests many highly successful strategies that are effective for coaching in all content areas. It has become one of the dog-eared books on my shelf as I am searching for more impactful ways to support those that I coach.

I have also found the expertise of Jim Knight in his 2011 book, *Unmistakable Impact: A Partnership Approach for Dramatically Improving Instruction*, to be invaluable when trying to understand how coaching plays a pivotal role in building capacity in teachers for student achievement. He provides a view of the big picture as well as the smaller view into the needs of a teacher in the classroom.

Authors Linda Gross Cheliotes and Marceta Fleming Reilly, in *Coaching Conversations: Transforming Your School One Conversation at a Time* (2010), provide examples of situations and strategies to use to make it easier to become effective in coaching for changed behaviors. They provide protocols that are easy to follow and can be used in multiple situations.

Results Coaching, The New Essential for School Leaders (2010), written by Kathryn Kee, Karen Anderson, Vicky Dearing, Edna Harris, and Frances Shuster, provides the "why" and the "how" for the need to change the way we work as school leaders. To be a facilitator of change, intentional changes in our language and communications skills are needed. From my initial introduction to Cognitive Coaching with Kee in GCISD in my role as a TOSA, to my current role in professional development, those skills are of value to me. I credit Kee with my skill set to be silent so I can hear to understand rather than use autobiographical listening, to use positive presuppositions about a person's intent, and to be thoughtful in my responses and questions so that they cause deeper thinking in those who have asked me to coach them.

Part III

STEM-ifying Instruction

A common question among educators considering a STEM focus is "How does STEM offer more specialized programs while still meeting the requirements of state standards and assessments?" STEM is about making learning more interesting and engaging. The content being learned in a STEM-based program is made more relevant to students by engaging in real-world problem-solving and exploring career connections with different types of engineering. When the focus is shifted, instruction becomes problem-solving and engineering.

12

Learning Through the Lens of STEM

The priorities of STEM-based learning are the continuous threads that run through planning, teaching, and learning. These priorities provide the instructional perspective about which instructional skills, strategies, and student actions are selected, utilized, and adapted daily for students' learning and academic growth. These are infused into the lesson by viewing it through the lens of STEM. The lens acts as a checklist to ensure they are included when planning the units of instruction and daily lessons:

◆ 21st Century Skills
◆ Career connections
◆ Global and real-world perspective
◆ Integrating technology
◆ Discourse and student voice
◆ Student choice and autonomy
◆ Giving and receiving feedback
◆ Interdisciplinary perspective
◆ Connecting literacy and authentic sources
◆ Involving the community and stakeholders.

A well-developed STEM unit of instruction takes into consideration the integration of all the components that make STEM different from traditional instruction. These include the practices of scientists and engineers, problem-based learning, engineering design, and differentiation for the needs of all learners.

21st Century Skills

Additional benefits of STEM-based learning are the interactions of students who are part of a design team. Students learn to communicate their ideas and to divide the workload. Incorporation of these 21st Century Skills is endorsed by Workforce development programs that recognize that such skills cannot be learned on the job, but need to be fully developed during the adolescent years.

Among the other 21st Century Skills based on the recent trends in Workforce development programs are those regarding collaboration in project completion, to be flexible and adaptive as they encounter failures in their plans and need to redesign, and to become innovative and creative as they try new approaches. The development of an open mindset becomes a focus of a STEM-centered program because of the benefits to students when being challenged to solve problems about which they have no prior experience: they have a willingness to experiment, to be inventive, to persist, and to try new ways of accomplishing a task.

Developing a sense of curiosity and wonder when faced with an unknown is a valuable skill. Using prior knowledge and calling on prior successes to design solutions, rather than using a prescribed step-by-step process, is a function of STEM. Encouraging students to be risk-takers with ideas and developing sound reasoning as they are choosing which path to take during inquiry encourages them to use higher-order thinking as they are defining problems, making decisions, and gaining skills in self-directing their choices.

Persistence and the willingness to accept a challenge even with the possibility of failure are dictated by a person's mindset. Carolyn Dweck describes the effects of students having fixed or a growth mindset in her book, *Mindset: The New Psychology of Success* (2006). The fear of being revealed as someone less than perfect, talented, or gifted—as many parents insist their children are— shows up as an unwillingness to try new challenges or to step outside the box. Dweck suggests that the development of an open mindset is possible and beneficial to the development of students' perspectives and skills that are needed to be successful in their lives and workplaces.

Within our classrooms that is a possibility, based on the way we provide feedback. When their work is judged by a growth rubric rather than an evaluation rubric a student can use the same criteria as their teacher to judge their work, performance, or products. They can determine their progression along a growth continuum. The standards of work range from novice, to gaining skill, to skillful, and to showing mastery. This standard of work, with criteria for each level, allows for a student to say, "I'm not there yet" rather than saying, "I'm a failure." Being given a letter grade declares they are a failure, passing, good, or excellent, proving their supposition that they were not talented or smart enough.

Technology integration and becoming technology literate are essential for students in the adult world. As Dr. Stotts from Educate Texas reminds us, "Our homes and our lives are driven by technology. We use it to solve our problems every day!" Wouldn't educators agree that we would be remiss to not allow students to utilize their personal technology? Its many functions can be used in our classrooms as they learn to solve problems and use the resources they have at hand.

When the view of technology expands to it being a tool that extends our abilities and our reach then we are no longer limited to the electronic device in the form of tablets, laptops, or cell phones. According to the Boston Museum of Science's Engineering Is Elementary (EIE) program, "Technology is anything made by humans to solve a problem; it can be an object, a system, or a process." The EIE lens gives STEM-focused classrooms the permission to invent technology and innovate from inventions to improve designs, build new ones, and solve problems in systems that do not require computers.

Additional 21st Century Skills identified by the Metiri Group include:

> digital age literacy, inventive thinking, interactive communication skills, high-quality and effective use of real tools. In a STEM-based classroom, many opportunities need to be planned for students to be engaged in authentic, inventive thinking that utilizes the communications skills of careful listening to understand another's perspective and thoughts. This also includes the ability for students to communicate their own ideas in a way that they are clearly understood and effective. Rarely are there opportunities in a traditional classroom for student discourse and argumentation. With a STEM lens toward teaching and learning, students are given more voice and choice in the way they communicate their understanding in their studies and the products they produce through their knowledge and skills.

Using Authentic Practices of Scientists and Engineers

A Framework for K-12 Science Education (NRC, 2012) addresses the needs of the science education community to re-evaluate the current science standards in use and the work students in science classes are doing. The National Research Council's findings indicate that the outdated ways current science education is preparing the future generation to meet the needs of our global economy would not be sufficient. It advocates new standards and new practices to prepare for the next generation of scientifically literate students to be college and career ready.

The findings written into *A Framework For K-12 Science Education* (2012) were based on research and documents produced prior to its publication. The research studies by the NRC included *How People Learn: Brain, Mind, Experience, and School* (1999), *America's Lab Report: Investigations In High School Science* (2005), and *Ready, Set, Science* (2008). They provided a compelling argument for the need for new standards and inclusion of scientific and engineering practices in the education of our students who are the next generation of global citizens.

Based on the NRC's findings, STEM education focuses on developing the skillful use and habits of mind that are authentic to the practices and ways of thinking by scientists and engineers. These practices are used as they answer questions about the phenomena of the natural world and design solutions to problems that are authentic to the real world. The practices of scientists and engineers are now part of the *Next Generation Science Standards* (Achieve, 2013).

The practices of scientists and engineers include:

◆ Asking questions and defining problems
◆ Developing and using models
◆ Planning and carrying out investigations
◆ Analyzing and interpreting data
◆ Using mathematics, information, and computer technology and computational thinking
◆ Constructing explanations and designing solutions
◆ Engaging in argument from evidence
◆ Obtaining, evaluating, and communicating information.

Being part of a STEM program means that the instructional strategies of a traditional classroom will no longer be effective in the implementation of science and math instruction. Integration of literacy skills such as reading, writing, listening, and speaking into all content areas should be the norm. Engineering and technology must be integrated into the learning and thinking patterns every day in the classroom as much as they are outside in the real lives of our students. And we must ask whether considerations for engaging students in age- and developmentally appropriate inquiry have become the priority in designing learning experiences.

Project-Based Learning

Project-based learning (PBL) is an instructional strategy that offers real-world applications of problem-solving skills and 21st Century Skills. PBL is aligned to content standards for a variety of content disciplines, allows students to try on authentic roles in many career fields, and requires the design of a solution that solves an authentic real-world problem. Students in collaborative groups can be given a broad range of autonomy in their pathways towards a solution and are given an opportunity to share their solutions in an array of venues and media. There are several components to PBL that make it a complex and sophisticated way of teaching: the integration of STEM content areas but also the overarching and underlying infusion of 21st Century Skills, instructional strategies that can be adapted to the diverse needs of the learners in the room, and it is based in the authentic practices of those who solve similar problems in the real world. For PBL to be more than a project the content knowledge and skill development is not front-loaded. These important components are learned through the completion of a PBL activity. The proficiency of the acquired knowledge and skills is seen through the presentation of the final product that is unique to each group of learners.

PBLs require a disproportionate amount of time for planning and preparation on the part of the teacher prior to the introduction of the PBL but then once the PBL has been released to the students, the teachers' time is spent facilitating, coaching, and monitoring student progress towards the engineering of the solution and the presentation of their work. The better the planning and preparation the higher caliber the student work becomes.

A PBL exercise is introduced usually through an entry event such as a newspaper article, a media clip of a real-world occurrence, or a contrived situation that is acted out by a local authority or the teacher. That is followed up by an entry document that provides an overview of the situation, the criteria and constraints of the solution, and a call to action to break into teams and begin brainstorming and designing a solution to the problem. The problem in need of a solution has a community or global perspective, requires pulling knowledge from other content areas, demands computational thinking, and means presenting the findings and solutions beyond the group.

It is the nature of each PBL activity to build interdependence between members of a student work group: it is structured so that each person in the group is identified as an expert in one aspect of the problem. For example, in a PBL exercise concerned with the erosion that is taking place in a neighborhood park, a local citizens group is seeking a solution to the problem that is sustainable, able to withstand annual flash flooding, is within a limited budget, and can be built with local products; the scheme needs to be completed by a certain date so it can be presented to a planning board meeting. Within each group of students there are roles found in authentic situations, such as a civil engineer, meteorologist, geologist, and landscape architect.

To build interdependence within the group, each of the roles is provided with a set of resources, and an explanation of what the role entails and the responsibilities towards the final presentation. It is each group member's responsibility to share with their team the information they were given, at the time it is appropriate. They are also encouraged to find additional information and resources through research and using authentic sources. There are many effective techniques for providing the experts their information as well as setting up a time line for completion of the scheme, with specific checkpoints along the way. Based on the ages and ability levels of the students, teacher coaching may be needed for these tasks.

Key to the success of PBL is the facilitation and coaching provided by the teacher and the feedback provided by rubrics. There are two rubrics that provide guidance to the groups along with the entry document. One rubric is the group rubric that is completed by the group through consensus at the end of the project. It allows for growth along a continuum from novice to expert. Items in the team rubric include: content knowledge, use of the engineering design process, team collaboration, and the quality of the product in meeting the criteria and constraints. The individual rubric focuses on one of the 21st Century Skills, such as: communication, presentation, innovation and creativity, integration of technology, and team collaboration. Students complete their own individual rubrics at the end of the project as well.

The rubrics break down each item into the criteria, allowing the student or group to rate it along the continuum. The value of such growth rubrics is that they point out specifically how a student's rating could improve to the next higher level by practicing or becoming more skillful in specific ways. For example, in the individual rubric for the 21st Century Skill of presentation the items that are to be evaluated are: eye contact and physical presence, speaking, organization, audio/visual aids, response to audience, and audience skills. These are located on the left side of the rubric. Across the top are the levels: expert, competent, gaining skill, and novice. For the speaking item, the criteria are, for novice: "Mumbles or speaks too softly to be heard. May mispronounce or use the wrong words. Uses phrases that are not appropriate for presentations." The criteria for the same item of speaking, at the expert level, are "Uses a variety of styles and changes pace to add interest to presentation. Pauses for dramatic effect and has a clear, loud voice with no filler phrases."

The audience for each of the presentations should have at least one other adult who can ask questions to check the students' understanding of their applicable knowledge and provide feedback to each group. This audience member provides some authenticity to the need for students to be accurate, rehearsed, and polished in their presentations.

Assessment is through several formats: the traditional unit assessment that can be open-ended or multiple choice, claim–evidence–reasoning responses related to the main ideas of PBL, and the accuracy in which they self-assess their levels of skills on the PBL rubrics. The rubrics for PBL are growth rubrics, which provide four levels of growth. As students rate their own level of proficiency in either content mastery or a 21st Century Skill such as presentation, collaboration, or creativity, they are able to determine where they are on a continuum from novice towards mastery. If they are not at mastery yet, they are provided feedback for what might be ways to gain skill and become more proficient. Rubrics do not necessarily provide grades, but do show growth.There are many sources for PBL exercises and training is available for creating and facilitating such STEM-centered learning. Sources include: www.Edutopia.com and the Buck Institute (www.BIE.org). Books that I used as I was learning to develop PBL are listed at the end of Part III.

Engineering Design

The "E" in STEM stands for engineering. Engineering involves design and systems thinking. These higher cognitive processes take into account all the parts that come into play within a system and the complex decisions that are made to make the system functional. The solution to a problem involves designing or innovating within the criteria and constraints of the problem. Although this sounds like something that should only be undertaken by mature problem-solvers, it is valuable for even the youngest of our students when given age-appropriate design challenges.

The role of engineering in a STEM program is the glue that makes it authentic. When students are engaged in the design process, creativity, innovation, thinking at a higher cognitive level, and gaining perspectives that take them outside the boundary of the places they live are involved. Engineering introduces systems thinking which develops within each student the ability to carefully consider the trade-offs and scientific reasoning to weigh the considerations when the choices are made.

Students examine the many parts of the system and determine how each part is connected, interconnected, and interacts with other parts. There are trade-offs that need to be made to stay within the constraints. Each individual decision comes with a need to weigh the impact a change to each part of the system will have on its overall ability to solve the problem. According to Marcela Borge in Chapter 4 of *Reconceptualizing STEM Education* (2016), "Though individuals in today's society need to be able to engage in systems thinking, support for the development of this type of reasoning is currently lacking." She goes on to state that as adults they will need this ability to carefully consider trade-offs between economic, cultural, and environmental demands.

The engineering component in science education is discussed in the National Research Council's *A Framework for K-12 Science Education* 1 (2012, page 12): engineering "provides a context in which students can test their own developing scientific knowledge and apply it to practical problems; doing so enhances their understanding of science—and for many, their interest in science—as they recognize the interplay among science, engineering, and technology." The NRC takes the stance that when students are engaged in the practices of engineering design they are learning science—engineering is as much a part of science as is engaging in the practices of scientists.

Setting up an engineering design experience is not as complex as setting up a PBL exercise, but it does have some of the same elements. While PBL exercises have a scenario and expert roles assigned to each team member, engineering design challenges require a division of labor, clear criteria and constraints, and a growth rubric for assessing the solution.

An engineering design experience requires more than just laying out the materials and saying, "Go!" To be an aligned part of instruction it needs to be based on the content standard, provide an opportunity to utilize the science content knowledge, seamlessly integrate the associated vocabulary, as well as build 21st Century Skills. Additionally, it should teach and use an engineering design process that includes individual as well as team skills, such as the skills to clarify the problem, define the criteria and constraints, imagine, brainstorm, research, plan, draw a prototype, build the prototype, test, evaluate, redesign, rebuild, retest, and present the solution.

Although these appear to be a list of steps, the engineering design process is a collection of skills that interact and build on each other. It is not a linear process and there are parts within the process that are reiterative, depending on where in the system failures first appear. Mindset is a factor in the students' dedication to the reiteration of redesigning, rebuilding, and retesting. Students with an open mindset do not see failure within the system as the end, but see it as just the first step within the design process to find a solution. But, students with a closed mindset find that they are blocked in their ability to continue to reiterate. They see their skills in design to be fixed and are not motivated to continue to redesign because of their way of thinking about their abilities. Facilitation and coaching by the teacher are key to helping students to change their mindsets and engineering solutions.

Design experiences such as building towers, bridges, roller coasters, and protective capsules for falling eggs are some of the first ones most teachers begin with. But many descriptive investigations of systems that require models to be able to explain or describe the components' structures and functions work well as engineering design experiences. An example of these could include creating a model of an animal from recycled materials that has structures and traits that are adaptions to its specific environment. Students have choice and voice in this project and it is not expected that each design is identical. Criteria and constraints include limiting the materials to those available in the classroom, justification for the selection of certain materials based on their properties needed for the adaptation of the animal to its environment, and a set timeframe for designing and building the animal.

The presentation by the design team needed to include the brainstorming design sketches, a sketch of the prototype initially built, a list of the design failures and innovations utilized, and finally the properties of each of the materials selected, the reasons why the animal structure was put together the way it was, and the functions of the animal's adaptation. The presentation and the model would be team-evaluated using the design rubric and self-evaluated using the 21st Century Skills rubric.

Engineering as part of a STEM campus and classroom provides a rich backdrop to the high levels of engagement, application of knowledge, cross-curricular connections, and infusion of 21st Century Skills that are essential to college and career readiness. In my experience with students and adults engaged in engineering design experiences, it is often difficult to call time because of the enjoyment, enthusiasm, and team-building that always occur with these experiences!

13

Integrating Other Content Area Standards into STEM

Integrating Literacy

The benefits of viewing literacy instruction through the STEM lens result from the ability of students to generalize literacy strategies to other non-fiction text. The practice of reading is genuine and provides an interdisciplinary approach to solving authentic, real-world problems. STEM literacy encompasses some instructional practices that are interwoven:

◆ Close reading skills for non-fiction complex text
◆ Vocabulary development of STEM and non-STEM words
◆ Communicating using the authentic forms of scientists and engineers
◆ Argumentation and discourse from a STEM perspective
◆ Writing in many formats for different audiences
◆ Producing and evaluating resources for authenticity and accuracy.

To accomplish STEM literacy considerable practice is needed in the selection of appropriate resources that will accomplish the dual purposes of providing content knowledge and giving a glimpse into the real world of scientists, engineers, and others who are using these skills in an authentic way.

Knowledge and expertise in literacy strategies are required for you to assist STEM teachers in making resources accessible to their students. Strategies for decoding text and close reading will require before, during, and after scaffolding to support developing and struggling readers. As students are selecting their own Internet resources, care should be taken to help them learn how to evaluate these resources for accuracy, expertise, as well as readability. Many resources are available to STEM teachers and, as their coach, if you are not familiar with how to locate them, you might gain more information about close reading strategies through the ELA lead teachers or specialists. As a STEM coach, your expertise in these strategies is essential if you are to be successful in guiding the interdisciplinary approach to STEM literacy.

Part of the global perspective of STEM is to provide access to the works of authentic writers and the primary documents of those in STEM fields. As a STEM coach it is necessary to ensure STEM teachers are exposing students to age-appropriate situations that have a need for designed solutions. STEM literacy is a way to use authentic text from a global perspective for the development of empathy in an age-appropriate way. Students show a sincere level of concern when asked to design engineering or social solutions for age-appropriate scenarios. By being provided with various perspectives into the solution, they see that life is complex, but they can contribute to making it sustainable.

Integrating Technology

Joe Todd, instructional specialist in technology in GCISD, says Google integration is on the horizon for the technology team and they plan to get Google certified. Others on the technology team are eager to learn how to integrate science probe ware. So, the technology team plans to learn from each other about how they can use Google to communicate the information gathered from science lab-based probe ware. Is this the approach and attitude of those within the STEM program in your district and classroom? As part of the vision for technology use in the STEM-centered classroom, has the authentic use of technology that mimics use by scientists, engineers, and other professionals been a consideration in the way the system was established and maintained?

Technology such as robotics programs and computer-based 3D printers is part of design thinking, although it may not be aligned to mastery of content standards. Often seen as the "T" in STEM, robotics programs are treated as elective courses and available to only a few students. Robotics can also be part of a STEM club that meets after school or on weekends with a limited number of members. When checking to see if your campus or classroom technology usage is part of an integrated STEM program it is important to examine how technology is being utilized. Is it a tool for problem-solving, gathering and processing information, and looking for ways to apply the standards-based content knowledge?

When designing STEM experiences for students, teachers need to consider how technology will be utilized in support of students gaining mastery of the standards for science and mathematics: not as a source for remediation software, but for uses authentic to STEM careers. Using lab probe ware for measurements may be the first opportunity for technology integration, providing connections to how these tools are used in authentic scientific and engineering pursuits in industry. Beyond using technology in lab investigations and gathering data as substitutes for non-electronic measuring tools, technology can be used in the analysis of data and observations. Generating data tables and pictorial representations of data in charts and graphs provides an opportunity to look for trends, and extrapolate trends to make predictions.

Technology is also the basis for the research needed for engineering design experiences and PBL activities to determine prior innovations, factors that may influence design decisions, as well as providing data and information needed for greater insights into the solution to the problem.

As digital natives who have grown up with technology, often your students are better versed in the use of the technology for these purposes. Teachers tend to be more cautious in their approach to online and networked systems. It is a disservice to students when technology use is limited to instructional purposes such as projecting information. When student technology use is seamless for information and data collecting, retrieval, processing, and analysis the integration of technology into the STEM environment is correctly designed.

Integrating Math

When designing houses that require integrated math and science content knowledge, you have the beginning of a STEM-shifted program. Staying within limiting constraints such as budgets and time as well as meeting the criteria of being energy efficient and eco-friendly adds to the authentic nature of the task. Authentic and real-world problems such as these that are aligned to content standards yet provide the opportunity for students to design solutions that have autonomy can show their understanding of what it means to be eco-friendly and energy efficient.

When teachers give each content area of a STEM-based lesson equal focus, students are engaged in rigorous problem-solving. Students use science as the basis for gaining a deeper level of understanding about how human activity can impact an environment. They are able to show that humans can still use resources in a manner that does not harm the environment, and keep them safe and abundant for other populations in an ecosystem. Students use mathematics to determine the differences in consumption of water and electricity, measure the differences in habitat disruption by surveying native species before and after human invasion, and compare by using statistics to determine the quality and costs of the materials used in the construction.

A Framework for K-12 Science Education points out that to be scientifically literate quantitative reasoning is required. STEM integration into science requires not just linking mathematics and engineering to science, but using math and engineering as a means to determining how reasonable the answer is and if it is feasible with the time and budget provided. This type of application requires the use of mathematical reasoning that goes beyond the numbers and unit labels used to report average energy and resource use. It represents the application of critical thinking and problem-solving that is authentic to scientists and engineers.

Recent research into the inclusion of mathematical concepts into STEM and science addresses the question of how to include quantitative reasoning rather than just measurement into STEM instruction. According to Anthony J. Petrosino in *Reconceptualizing STEM Education* (2016), there are recommendations for integrating a conceptual understanding of math models "that are based on an established and ever growing body of research on how people solve problems, design, reason, and learn disciplinary contexts."

Students have an opportunity to apply mathematical concepts and understandings to real-world problems when sampling, distribution, or variability of data are taught when doing investigations, design challenges, or PBLs in STEM programs. Collecting data that are messy and complex is important for students so that they experience how to analyze it. It is a disservice to STEM students to simply disregard the outliers and average the data sets. By including the development of a mathematical conceptual understanding in these STEM pursuits while the engagement is high and the interest in mathematical reasoning is genuine, students will relish the insights of how engineers, scientists, and those in career fields make their decisions in authentic ways.

Katy ISD's math–science instructional coach Marisa Guzman's goal is for students to solve authentic problems like the ones they find every day, but not just using science or math, but also using the lens of engineering. The combined processes they use to solve complex and sophisticated, yet age-appropriate, problems will become the skills that they will be prepared to use in designing solutions and solving problems in their future lives and careers. That is STEM. STEM is about being prepared for a career and earning a living. That is economics.

Current and future jobs are being created in the areas of technology and engineering. In Guzman's opinion, these careers are project based and the professionals in them will use their backgrounds in science and math content in them. To learn the content in engaging and hands-on ways her students are participating in well-designed work that is team- and content-based. It is critical for them to learn to work together to complete their projects. They learn math and science while they are engaged in design projects. They also learn how to work together. In Guzman's opinion it is important to learn these skills now for use in their future jobs. Future careers will require employees to collaborate with others and to solve problems as a team.

As the math–science instructional coach Guzman finds that engineering is the perfect way to learn how *A Framework for K-12 Science* (NRC, 2012) looks at integrating engineering. And Guzman works with teachers to understand how the *Next Generation Science Standards* (NRC, 2013) brings STEM all together to problem solve and to participate in challenging tasks. They plan lessons together for their students to use an engineering design process (EDP), collecting data, asking questions, and sharing results with everyone.

Guzman provides a STEM lens for concepts being taught to add a real-world perspective and relevance to the lessons being presented. For example, when a teacher might be uncomfortable with fractions and asks for her to model the lesson for her, Guzman looks over the resources she has and uses manipulatives and materials. For example, she may model an authentic problem for students to solve using inquiry and a constructivist approach. Guzman chose a specific task just before a holiday break when the office staff needed to make a certain number of bows out of a limited amount of ribbon for the gifts they were giving to volunteers. Each group of students had their own method and ideas of how to do it. So she gave them three and a half yards of ribbon and the number of bows that were needed. Then each group developed and shared their plans. Through a class discussion the students figured out which plan would work best. According to Guzman, "I provide the materials and manipulatives to show how to use real-world context to make it authentic. I can model it once; she gets it, and runs with it."

Differentiated Instruction and Age-Appropriate Strategies

Many teachers believe that students in elementary school cannot solve their own problems or design solutions to engineering challenges. According to Denise Fisher, K-12 STEM coach in Texarkana ISD, "A kindergarten student can do so much more than their teachers think they can do." By using deep questioning and scaffolding in the math and science concepts, students enjoy the rigor and go further than just getting their feet wet and surface learning. She stated that when teachers know how to use inquiry, students engage and learn to ask the questions as they solve the problems.

The purpose of STEM, as described in *A Framework for K-12 Science Education* (NRC, 2012, page 277), is to help ensure and evaluate educational equity. "Concerns about equity should be at the forefront of any effort to improve the goals, structures, and practices that support learning and educational attainment for all students." It goes on to discuss how, just as students are expected to learn to read and write, all students should be expected to learn core ideas and the practices of science and engineering as the basis for scientific literacy.

Instructional decisions and differentiated strategies based in education research make it possible to adapt lessons, STEM experiences, and expected outcomes and products. For these to be appropriate to the background knowledge, experiences, abilities, and interests of the students teacher differentiation is required. According to the *Framework* (page 280) "All individuals, with a small number of notable exceptions, can engage in and learn complex subject matter … When supportive conditions and feedback mechanisms are in place and the learner makes a sustained effort." STEM experiences lend themselves to differentiation and adaptation because of the open-ended expectations for student success. By providing for choice and voice and growth rubrics, students have an opportunity to grow from where they are to where they need to be through the appropriate instructional strategies and adapted resources provided.

Part III

Summary, Conclusion, and Resources

STEM-ification of traditional science, math, and other content areas is possible with an open mindset and the desire to prepare students in the most effective way possible. Transitioning to these practices requires the support and encouragement of someone who is knowledgeable and experienced in their use.

Using the authentic practices of scientists, engineers, and those in related professional roles makes the learning more engaging and opens students' vistas to prepare for a STEM-based career. Project-based learning, engineering design, and the integration of literacy, math, and technology are not optional for a STEM program.

Part IV provides a view into the necessary supports and components of a STEM campus. STEM coaches are an integral part in helping campus leadership move forward in this process.

Resources

References

Achieve, Inc. (2013). *Next Generation Science Standards* (NGSS). Washington, DC: National Academies Press, ngss.nsta.org/PracticesFull.aspx

Borge, Marcela (2016). Systems Thinking as a Design Problem. In Richard A. Duschl and Amber S. Bismack, (Eds.), *Reconceptualizing STEM Education*. New York: Routledge.

Dweck, Carolyn (2006*). Mindset: The New Psychology of Success*. New York City, NY: Ballantine Books.

National Research Council (NRC) (1999). *How People Learn: Brain, Mind, Experience, and School*. Washington, DC: National Academies Press.

National Research Council (NRC) (2005). *America's Lab Report: Investigations in High School Science*. Washington, DC: National Academies Press.

National Research Council (NRC) (2008). *Ready, Set, Science*. Washington, DC: National Academies Press.

National Research Council (NRC) (2012). *A Framework for K-12 Science Education*. Washington, DC: National Academies Press.

Petrosino, Anthony J. (2016). Teachers' Use of Data, Measurement, and Data Modeling in Quantitative Reasoning. In Richard A. Duschl and Amber S. Bismack (Eds.), *Reconceptualizing STEM Education*. New York: Routledge.

STEM Summer Leadership Institute (2015). *Rewiring School Culture*, www.tstemblueprint.org/artifacts/

References for PBL

Boss, Suzie (2013). *PBL for 21st Century Success: Teaching Critical Thinking, Collaboration, Communication, and Creativity*. Novato, CA: Buck Institute for Education.

Capraro, Robert M. and Slough, Schott W. (2009). *Project-Based Learning: An Integrated Science, Technology, Engineering and Mathematics (STEM) Approach*. Rotterdam: Sense Publishers.

Hallermann, Sara, Larmer, John, and Mergendoller, John R. (2011). *PBL in the Elementary Grades: Step-By-Step Guidance, Tools and Tips for Standards-Focused K-5 Projects*. Novato, CA: Buck Institute for Education.

Larmer, John, Ross, David, and Mergendoller, John R. (2009). *PBL Starter Kit: To the Point Advice, Tools and Tips for Your First Project in Middle or High School*. Novato, CA: Buck Institute for Education.

Markham, Thom, Larmer, John, and Ravitz, Jason (2003). *Project-Based Learning: A Guide to Standards-Focused Project-Based Learning for Middle and High School Teachers*. Novato, CA: Buck Institute for Education.

Port, Linda and Sage, Sara (2002). *Problems as Possibilities: Problem-Based Learning for K-16 Education*, 2nd Edition. Alexandria, VA: ASCD.

Organization Websites

The Metiri Group—www.metiri.com
www.Edutopia.com
Buck Institute—www.BIE.org
Texas STEM Coalition—www.txstem.org

Part IV

Transforming to a STEM-Based Campus

As you consider the role of the STEM coach in the transition process, there are many opportunities that can build on the excitement for the district, campus, classroom, and community. Some are obvious but others are easily overlooked. In this final part of the *Handbook* a broad brushstroke is applied to the many tasks needed for the transition of a traditional campus to a STEM-based one and the important role the STEM coach plays in it.

14

STEM Coach and Campus Transformation

Felecia Pittman, STEM coach from the UT Dallas T-STEM Center, provided support to the campuses she served as they were working to change the culture to embrace STEM and a STEM mindset. She partnered with campus leaders in finding strategic alliances, and establishing relationships with community and university partners. In her administrator coaching sessions Pittman discussed the need to create an advisory board:

> Gaining ground on some of the T-STEM Design Blueprint benchmark items was very hard for most campuses. I was there to support, provide examples, and help to generate ideas. I attended all their STEM advisory council meetings. Creating a STEM culture was a challenge. We worked on planning how it looks on the campus and what does that look like in the portrait of their academy STEM graduates. We worked on what they should share with the public in campus newsletters, stationery, and on their website. The website was their vehicle for outreach. Image may not have been as critical in a one-campus town but when a STEM academy is a school-of-choice, it needed to portray the campus as a viable option for student achievement and success through STEM.

STEM-Based Transformation to a STEM Culture

Once the culture of the STEM-based campus has shifted to one where learning is the focus and student growth is the indicator of success the community will see many significant changes. There will be integrated studies blended into mastery learning of the standards through hands-on authentic problems and solutions. Students will be thinking globally about the impact of their solutions. 21st Century Skills are part of the learning process and students will be fluent in the literacy skills that link STEM to the real world and the community. The shift to STEM will create new ways of thinking about teaching and learning, as well as bringing the authentic world inside the classroom. It is the potential of the STEM graduate who will be an integral part of the community that requires a STEM campus to open their doors and invite the community and business stakeholders to join them in the development and growth of the students who will be joining their ranks.

Shifting the culture of the campus to a STEM campus requires the following, outlined in the 2015 STEM Summer Leadership Institute's *Rewiring School Culture*:

1. Understanding the concept of STEM: what it is and what it is not
2. Understanding the culture of STEM: recognizing leverage points, roadblocks, recognizing the current status, and past successes and issues
3. Shaping a new culture: describing the change, building the capacity to change, building a team mindset, and appreciating what is working well.

The T-STEM Design Blueprint (2015) and the supporting documents for the development of a STEM culture can be found on the T-STEM website, designed to support campuses in their transition to becoming STEM.

STEM Stakeholders

Lancaster ISD, in northeast Texas, is a Texas Education Agency (TEA) T-STEM district. This unique situation came about because of a series of conversations between district, industry, and community leaders. Based on a need for industry workers, who are skilled enough to step into STEM-based jobs, and want to live in the community to help it grow, the district evaluated the role science played in the successful employment of graduates in the region. In the past, little value was placed on science instruction; it was not always taught at the elementary level and lacked rigorous or advanced instruction at the high school level. Area graduates were not qualified for local employment in the STEM-based industries nor did they pursue STEM-based degrees or careers.

With the endorsement of area stakeholders and the support of industry leaders, such as Texas Instruments, Lancaster ISD applied for and received STEM-designation. Science instruction needed to be energized and the stakeholders needed to be kept apprised of the changes that would be occurring in the school system. STEM provided the foundation for changing the culture and learning environment of the district. Science and 21st Century Skills were going to be the foundation for their STEM program.

The district's new superintendent and administration team developed a vision for science that includes partnering with parents and industry as stakeholders. The change started from the top down, with administration, rather than bottom up, from the teachers. This initiative was massive, so the STEM-designated district was assigned a T-STEM coach to work with district leadership as they developed a new structure to support campuses and teachers. For this level of change to happen, campuses needed to be supported with resources, training, coaching, and monitoring. It was also important to educate the community and parents so they could anticipate and look forward to the changes that were going to happen in the classrooms.

STEM Events

As a means to keep the community and stakeholders informed and excited about the benefits and growth of the STEM program, holding campus and community STEM events provides a venue to showcase student achievement. On a traditional campus, parent groups such as a parent–teacher association (PTA) are tasked to provide venues for parents to support the campus. However, on a STEM campus parental participation is through the lens of being stakeholders in the celebration of students' success towards their future college and career readiness. At a STEM campus, student learning and thinking is at the heart of campus events. Concerts, art shows, STEM fairs, parent STEM nights, and robotics competitions have replaced the more traditional events of the past.

When embracing STEM strategies and the development of 21st Century Skills, students become the organizers, presenters, and agents for change that reflects their value and contribution to the community. The community in turn will work to provide resources for the STEM campus's growth. Although many STEM campuses would appreciate monetary support from industry, it is the endorsement by community leaders, businesses, and industry that see the value of STEM-based instruction that will help to provide resources to help the STEM mindset to permeate the community.

STEM Community Includes Advisory Boards, Mentors, and an Authentic Audience

STEM is based in the authentic practices of the careers found in the real world. Stakeholders and community members play a valuable role in helping the STEM campus meet its goals. Being among people in STEM fields provides the real-world context that is needed to help students create their own vision of being part of the professional world. Part of the instructional practice of STEM is inviting the community to come into the classroom to share some of the age-appropriate issues they are grappling with that need solutions.

These problems will generate in students a passion to design and creatively tackle the process of finding the solution. Having authentic problems then allows for having members of the community be mentors and advisors who provide additional information, challenges, and resources. And when the team of students has designed its potential solutions, the mentor provides feedback about the product that will allow them to continue to grow in their abilities and capacities to solve problems.

A campus STEM advisory board, or STEM advisory council, is made up of stakeholders and community members who support the STEM initiative of the campus and work to keep it viable and focused on the targets of a STEM program. By asking the advisory board to actively participate in making decisions, they will provide the "outside of the school house" perspective that is vital to keeping STEM authentic and aligned to meeting the instructional standards and the community needs for college- and career-ready graduates.

STEM Mission and Vision

Being part of a STEM program provides a sense of pride and accomplishment for students as they push through the added expectations of math, science, and technology. They know that STEM is more than computer usage, engineering challenges, and enrolling in college-prep classes. Their enrollment in a STEM program is their first steps towards a promising future where STEM literacy is the way they make decisions, participate in their community, and provide for their futures.

The vision and mission of a STEM campus reflects the beliefs of those who work to shape the future of their STEM scholars. Campus leadership and the STEM advisory council craft a call to action that leads the campus forward in the development of the vision and mission statements. Once written, they become the lens through which all decisions are viewed and made for the continued achievement of the STEM students.

STEM Logo

The logo that symbolizes the goals and tenets of the STEM campus should be designed into a logo for the STEM campus. It should incorporate the vision of the campus as well as provide an identifier which the students use as a reminder of the investment they are making in their futures. Often STEM campuses display their logo on their website, the marquee to the school, and on stationery and publications sent out by the campus administration.

A logo displayed in prominent locations as visitors enter the campus clearly makes a statement about the caliber and integrity of work being done by students and teachers who are learning the skills of future problem-solvers and designers.

Sharing STEM Success with Others

The successes and transitions of STEM students should be shared with the community. Supporters in the community want to hear how much progress is being made and will join in the celebrations of student success.

Websites, newsletters, and articles in the community newspaper provide space for parents and community members to share in the positive climate the STEM campus achieves. Having the mission, vision, and logo on all the correspondence, newsletters, and the campus website provides that branding that is a push for continuing the transition and adjustments needed to become fully STEM focused, and to meet the expectations of the community for its graduates.

Part IV

Summary, Conclusion, and Resources

This final part of *The STEM Coaching Handbook* provides a larger view of a STEM campus's role and support in the community. As a means of connecting and communicating the importance of STEM literacy and college and career readiness, being identified as a STEM campus is important. As a STEM coach, you will be leading the charge in the organization, development, and maintenance of the new structure. Shifting the culture of a campus to being STEM focused is a challenging but rewarding task. Being part of a network of other STEM coaches provides a wealth of ideas and resources that you can use as you focus on the ideals and goals of your STEM program.

Resources

Websites

T-STEM Design Blueprint, www.tstemblueprint.org/
T-STEM Blueprint Artifacts, www.tstemblueprint.org/artifacts/

15

Final Thoughts

In closing, I would like to share some final thoughts from the coaches and administrators who shared their wisdom and advice with me in the preparation of *The STEM Coaching Handbook*.

Kyndra Johnson, director of STEM and Curriculum Innovation in Lancaster ISD, Lancaster, TX

I think the first bit of advice I would give is to get over yourself. We get in our own way sometimes. It doesn't matter about you. It matters about the teachers and campuses you are supporting. As a coach you need to be a continuous life-long learner by listening to and really hearing someone else's perspective. Share your experiences only to the point that it helps them to think through their decisions. Many times coaches think that because you are from central office you are going to manage or be over someone—but you are not, you are here to work. As a coach you need to be flexible and adaptable. You may be asked to work at a conference, or co-teach. The key is to be willing, open, and flexible in your role.

Jodi Marchesso, science instructional specialist, Pasadena USD, Pasadena, CA

I think for a coach—never stop learning yourself. Continue your own PD while providing PD for others; keep reading and searching for resources. This is hard to do because you spend all your time helping teachers. It is easy to forget to continue your own growth and development. The hardest part about being a coach is you are trying to change someone's beliefs. As a teacher you can always tell students what they need to know or do. But as a coach you need to help someone to see that what he or she is doing needs to change. It takes time. You may not see the change right away and you may get discouraged. But, it is important for you to believe that what you are doing is making a difference for the students you serve.

You can't be a coach without the ability to build a relationship. Teachers have no reason to believe you. We know that if you don't have a relationship with a student they won't be interested in what you have to say. The same is true with adult learners.

Dr. Leslie Hancock, onsite instructional coach, Grapevine-Colleyville ISD, Grapevine, TX

Just as every child needs a champion, every teacher needs a champion; an advocate, a thinking partner. They deserve a colleague who will hold up a mirror to their teaching strengths and engage in critical conversations, leading them to further professional evolution.

Denise Fisher, former K-12 STEM coach and STEM coordinator, Texarkana ISD, Texarkana, TX and currently GCISD learning liaison

My advice to someone who wants to be a STEM coach is to maintain your focus on STEM integration as your goal. You need to know what STEM looks like across a campus and if it matches what the district want their program to be. Unless they can articulate the why, the program will have no depth. You need to be sure they have the capacity for the changes required and that they are willing to support your efforts as they go through the growing pains.

Once it becomes the campus's goal, it is your only goal and you need to stay focused. Don't let anybody push it backwards or water it down. Continue to keep the bar high to meet the *STEM Blueprint* standards for a role-model campus. Even if you miss your goal, your students will be ten times richer for what they have learned.

Dr. Jennifer Stotts, STEM consultant and T-STEM coach with Educate Texas

Do your homework. Coaching is not easy when it is done well and when you consider the individual needs of each client. You need to assess where they are, and then plan with them how to get where they need to go along the STEM growth continuum. Keep learning. You cannot coach well if you don't keep up with the education and STEM research. Keep your finger on the pulse of the trends in your state's education initiatives.

Marisa Guzman, math–science STEM coach, Katy ISD, Katy, TX

My advice to a new STEM coach is to be knowledgeable. Keep up with your reading about the changes in curriculum and teaching strategies. Roll up your sleeves and do the work. It is better to prepare and prevent than to repair and repent. When you show up to your planning sessions and you are not prepared they see that as a weakness. You need to always be a step ahead.

Dr. John Doughney, executive director of learning in Grapevine-Colleyville ISD, Grapevine, TX

There is a big difference in coaching. As educators we want to help and fix. That is our job; those are rigid pathways in the brain that have developed over the course of our lives. But when you go into a coaching role that says your job is not to tell, there are a lot of habits that you have to consider and stop. So to truly coach, you have to take yourself out of the role of advisor, teller, and fixer. You truly must have the belief that for most people the answer is inside. You need to mediate their thinking to a higher level of thought and a higher level of performance.

Cindy Rubin, STEM consultant with Current Instruction

Be reflective. Many teachers think they don't have the time. If it is not built into their teaching day, they cannot find the time. We as coaches feel we need to free up the time for them to think about the issues. Don't pressure teachers to admit it was their fault. They understand that there are gaps, but it is up to you to help them close the gaps. Coaching helps them to think more deeply about their goals and to reflect on the strategies and practices important to move forward.

Dillon Chevalier, former T-STEM coach, UT Dallas, T-STEM Center, Dallas, TX

Work to create relationships built on trust and respect. By acknowledging their expertise, teachers are more comfortable taking ownership and making instructional decisions. Be a sounding board for them, but know when to add input or give advice that will move the learning process forward. Be humble and have humility.

Sara Jones, science curriculum and instructional coach, Harmony Public Schools, Houston, TX

As teachers, we differentiate our instruction to meet our students where they are. As a coach, you still have to think and act like a teacher but shift your approach to what works for adult learners. Like a teacher, you have to differentiate your coaching to meet your teachers where they are. You have to build a relationship with your teachers, just like you did with your students, before any work can begin. I approach each teacher differently, based on their personality and teaching style.

At the start of the year, I ask to meet with new teachers to explain my role and find out what they need. After that, I spend time in their classrooms. I go in announced and unannounced for quick walkthroughs and give feedback on positive things first. Through observing, I collect data to get to know their teaching style and see their strengths and weaknesses. I ask questions and based on their responses and what I have observed, I start to ask more probing questions that encourage reflection and make suggestions on how to improve instruction. I do different things with my returning teachers. Since we already have a relationship, we set new goals each year and continue working where we left off.

The needs of teachers vary greatly. Some teachers need guidance on classroom management, others on building relationships with students, and others on best practices. As long as you have a relationship in place, and meet teachers where they are, growth will happen. You have to remember that the goal of coaching is to improve instruction for students. The best part of my job is sharing best practices, seeing teachers grow and in turn, seeing student achievement increase.

Kristi Adams, STEM consultant with St. Gregory's University and former STEM coach with K20 STEM at the University of Oklahoma, Norman, OK
One of the hardest decisions I ever made in my career was to leave the classroom—but I could not have achieved where I am career-wise and built the relationships with teachers I have today, if I did not leave the classroom. I am exponentially reaching more students. It took me a while to figure that out and accept it. I am still focused on students. I am just going to get to them in a different way: through the way their teachers think, through their teaching, and the exceptional lessons they plan. I will still have an impact on students.

You may not change their thinking, but you have influenced them. You have planted a seed. It may be five years before it blossoms and they implement it. At the end of methods classes they were not ready to begin using it yet, but then five years down the road they contact you, to say they tried it with that one student who needed that one specific strategy—and it worked! That is teacher self-efficacy!

Felecia Pitman, T-STEM leadership coach, UT Dallas T-STEM Center, Dallas, TX

I like some of Janet Morrison's work of STEM. Many think adding robotics is STEM. The campus where I now work is implementing it on our campus; we modified the *Blueprint* and use it as a guide. Coaches need to visit lots of STEM campuses. Go into it knowledgeable and don't enter it from a naïve point of view. Go to Region 10 training and look for grants. Contact people who know more than you do. Keep an open mind, some of the things leaders say you will find interesting but it is apparent they need a larger definition of STEM. They give in to doing a lot of activities. The problem is they do not have a true STEM focus.

A few district people and administrators felt they could train their teachers themselves, but it was not as beneficial. Rather than sending their STEM teachers to STEM sources for information, they tried to do it in-house. Without an informed understanding of STEM they did not fully develop their program, they needed a broader picture before they started making their plans.

Kimberly Lane, technology instructional coach, Lancaster ISD, Lancaster, TX

Don't feel bad when you go home at night that you haven't conquered anything. Take things day by day. Don't be afraid to ask for help. Develop a PLN (personal learning network) with other coaches. I am the networking queen, I'd preach it all the time; learn from others. You can always get good information from others. Connect with other people and learn from them.

Joe Todd, STEM technology interventionist, Grapevine-Colleyville, ISD, Grapevine, TX

Two things come to mind, priorities and time, as I consider what I do as a coach:

1. Priorities. It is important to know what the top priorities are and to know what you should commit to and need to perhaps put off to next year. It needs to be a list of few but important priorities so that you can focus. Those priorities need to be crafted into your role in discussion with your administrator. I have my priorities posted above my desk in my cubicle as a daily reminder.
2. Time—how you use it when working with others and how they use your time. The usage of time needs to be thought through and planned. Time is a commodity that there is never enough of. So to make it beneficial to teachers and administration, you need to know

where it falls in the list of priorities so you can determine how much time to commit to it. I ask myself, "How much time can I commit to your project or question?" I consider for what amount of time will you use it with students and if you will continue to use it. We can't do it all so based on your priorities, you determine how you will spend your limited time.

As a coach, it is important to focus on the developmental needs of the adult learner as compared to the learning needs for the children and young adults for mastering the standards. The developmental needs of adults are about their pedagogy that is expressly beyond the content. A coach needs a good understanding of brain theory—to know why it would be needed to do this, unlike when you are teaching students. The research needs to be communicated to them so they see why they need to adopt a new approach to teaching.

When I was a swimming coach trying to teach adults to swim, I had to talk at a different level with them than with kids. They wanted to know the physics and anatomy & physiology of swimming and what they were specifically doing, to help them to understand why we swim in this way. It is important in helping adults to know the reasoning and research behind "why" the changes you are helping them to use are of benefit to student learning.

You have to respect the artist in the classroom. You are bringing your expertise to help them adopt the program but you should also be encouraging and supporting them to continue to be successful in meeting the needs of their students in their content area.

Dr. Terry Talley, STEM coach and program manager for Professional Development

Coaching and mentoring are two of the most rewarding experiences in my life. My dream of being an educator was to leave a legacy in education that would impact generations to come. When I can step into the role of mentor or coach and help someone realize their dream in shaping the futures of the students and teachers they serve, I know I am living my dream.

I hope the information and insights shared in *The STEM Coaching Handbook* are of value to you as you mentor and coach those you serve.

References

Achieve, Inc. (2013). *Next Generation Science Standards* (NGSS). Washington, DC: National Academies Press.

Borge, Marcela (2016). Systems Thinking as a Design Problem. In Duschl, Richard A. and Bismack, Amber S. (Eds.), *Reconceptualizing STEM Education*. New York: Routledge.

Dweck, Carolyn (2006). *Mindset: The New Psychology of Success*. New York City, NY: Ballantine Books.

Erickson, Lynn (2008). *Stirring the Head, Heart, and Soul: Redefining Curriculum, Instruction, and Concept-Based Learning*. Thousand Oaks, CA: Corwin Press.

Frontier, Tony and Rickabaugh, James (2014). *Five Levers to Improve Learning: How to Prioritize for Powerful School Results*. Alexandria, VA: ASCD.

Heath, Chip and Heath, Dan (2010). *Switch: How to Change Things When Change Is Hard*. New York: Broadway Books.

Hord, Shirley M., Rutherford, William L., Huling-Austin, Leslie, Hall, Gene E., and Knoll, Marcia Kalb (1987; revd 2006). *Taking Charge of Change*. Alexandria, VA: ASCD.

Kee, Kathryn, Anderson, Karen, Dearing, Vicky, Harris, Edna, and Shuster, Frances (2010). *Results Coaching, the New Essential for School Leaders*. Thousand Oaks, CA. Corwin Press & LearningForward

Knight, Jim (2011). *Unmistakable Impact: A Partnership Approach for Dramatically Improving Instruction*. Thousand Oaks, CA: Corwin Press & LearningForward.

National Research Council (NRC) (1999). *How People Learn: Brain, Mind, Experience, and School*. Washington, DC: National Academies Press.

National Research Council (NRC) (2005). *America's Lab Report: Investigations in High School Science*. Washington, DC: National Academies Press.

National Research Council (NRC) (2008). *Ready, Set, Science*. Washington, DC: National Academies Press.

National Research Council (NRC) (2012). *A Framework for K-12 Science Education*. Washington, DC: National Academies Press.

Petrosino, Anthony J. (2016). Teachers' Use of Data, Measurement, and Data Modeling in Quantitative Reasoning. In Duschl, Richard A. and Bismack, Amber S. (Eds.), *Reconceptualizing STEM Education*. New York: Routledge.